CLASSICS IN ANTHROPOLOGY

Rodney Needham, *Editor*

PRIMITIVE MARRIAGE

John F. McLennan   *1827–81*

PRIMITIVE MARRIAGE
An Inquiry into the Origin of the Form
of Capture in Marriage Ceremonies

JOHN F. McLENNAN

Edited and with an Introduction by
PETER RIVIÈRE

THE UNIVERSITY OF CHICAGO PRESS
CHICAGO & LONDON

J. F. McLennan's text originally was published in 1865
by Adam and Charles Black, Edinburgh.

International Standard Book Number: 0-226-56080-5
Library of Congress Catalog Card Number: 72-111602

The University of Chicago Press, Chicago 60637
The University of Chicago Press, Ltd., London
© 1970 by The University of Chicago
All rights reserved
Published 1970

Printed in the United States of America

Contents

v

CONTENTS

Editor's Introduction

W HETHER we have hit the truth or not, we trust we have at least been preparing the way for those who in the fulness of time will reach it."

John Ferguson McLennan wrote these words one hundred years ago in the opening pages of his article "The Worship of Animals and Plants," [1] and he would perhaps have been surprised to discover how far in the future the "fulness of time" lay, astonished that he had been the founder of a subject he did not recognize, and gratified that certain of his ideas still lingered on. But however far back one traces the origin of anthropological thought, McLennan represents an all important stage in its modern development because it is with him that the continuing topics of anthropological concern such as marriage forms, incest, exogamy (he coined the word), and totemism originated. *Primitive Marriage* was McLennan's first statement of his revolutionary ideas, and thus there is no need to explain or defend its republication in a series on classics in anthropology. Its qualification as a classic is indisputable since today's anthropologists are still heirs to McLennan's genius. Who was this man who founded a subject? The outline of his life is straightforward and easily told.

I

McLennan was born on 14 October 1827 in the Scottish highland town of Inverness, the eldest of three brothers. His father, John McLennan, was an insurance agent working for the Sea Insurance Association, and his mother was Jessie Ross McLennan. He went to school in Inverness and then to King's College, Aberdeen, in 1845; and he graduated from that university with an M.A. in 1849. At that time the curriculum of the four-year M.A. course consisted of: first year, Latin and

1. McLennan 1869c, p. 408, n. 1. A bibliography of McLennan's writings follows the Editor's Introduction.

Greek; second year, chemistry, mathematics, Latin and Greek; third year, natural philosophy, mathematics, Latin and Greek; fourth year, moral philosophy, logic, rhetoric, Latin and Greek.[2] He appears to have been an able mathematician; for in 1849 he was awarded both the Hutton and Simpson prizes for mathematics.[3] In 1848 he had become the secretary of the university's newly formed debating society.[4]

From Aberdeen McLennan moved to Cambridge University in 1849, and "there, in the first instance, he was entered at one of the lesser colleges (Caius and Gonville), but was immediately after his arrival invited to migrate to Trinity."[5] His tutor at Trinity College was the Plato scholar W. H. Thompson,[6] and his friends were mainly those with literary and philosophical interests, prominent among them being the essayist and Trinity librarian George Brimley.[7] However, he continued to show a flair for mathematics, and in 1853 he obtained a twenty-fifth Wrangler's place in the Tripos. He left Cambridge in the same year without bothering to take his degree.[8]

His activities during the next two years, 1853–55, are rather obscure, but he passed them in London engaged in literary and journalistic work, and perhaps in studying law.[9] He is

2. P. J. Anderson, *The Arts Curriculum* (Aberdeen: Printed for the Class of 1868–72, 1892), p. 14.

3. *List of Persons Admitted to the Degree of Master of Arts in the University and King's College of Aberdeen from the Year 1800 Inclusive* (Aberdeen: Printed by William Bennett, 1856), p. 45.

4. Private correspondence from Mr. A. T. Hall, deputy librarian, University Library, King's College, Aberdeen. Information from the university records.

5. "J. F. M'Lennan," an obituary, *The Scotsman* (Monday, 20 June 1881), p. 4. One would like to know who invited him and why.

6. W. W. Rouse Ball and J. A. Venn, *Admissions to Trinity College, Cambridge, 1801–1850* (London, 1911), p. 649.

7. Obituary, *The Scotsman*, p. 4.

8. J. R. Tanner, ed., *The Historical Register of the University of Cambridge* (Cambridge, 1917), p. 512. Perhaps he did not take his degree because he was dissatisfied with the Tripos result. He later mentioned to Lubbock that he would have done much better at Cambridge if he had not suffered from poor health (*Avebury Papers*, British Museum ms. 49641, letter from McLennan to Lubbock, dated 6 January 1870).

9. It was at this time that McLennan met William Michael Rossetti, and the latter described the Scotsman as "a rather 'gawky' young man,

reputed to have contributed to *The Leader* which was edited by George Lewes (together with Thornton Leigh Hunt) until 1854 when Lewes ran off with George Eliot.[10] McLennan was acquainted with these three, but his circle of friends also included such prominent literary figures as Alexander Munro, William Michael Rossetti, and Alexander Macmillan, the last just starting his publishing concern and who was to publish all of McLennan's later works.[11]

From London McLennan went back to Scotland, to Edinburgh as a law student where he lived with Alexander Smith, the Scottish poet, at 25 India Street.[12] Soon after his return to Scotland McLennan wrote to Rossetti saying that he had heard that he was to get a professorship for which he had applied.[13] His hopes proved unfounded, and we do not even know the whereabouts of the chair for which he unsuccessfully applied. He was called to the Scottish bar in January 1857, and

---

with a tall throat and prominent features the reverse of regular." (*Some Reminiscences* [London: Brown Langham & Co., 1906], p. 170.) Rossetti's description is admirably born out by McLennan's bust (see frontispiece).

10. *Dictionary of National Biography,* herafter cited as *DNB.* I have examined the volumes of *The Leader* for the years 1853–55 but have been unable to identify any article which could be unhesitatingly attributed to McLennan. Nor have I found any other writings of McLennan which date from this period, but Rossetti (*Reminiscences,* p. 170) refers to a collection of verses by McLennan entitled *Poems on the Praeraphaelite Principle,* and Professor W. E. Fredeman of the University of British Columbia who drew my attention to this reference informed me that a copy of this work was bound into one of Rossetti's "Miscellanies Prose and Poetry," dated 1855. Mrs. Imogen Dennis, the granddaughter of Rossetti, was kind enough to allow me to examine her grandfather's "Miscellanies," but McLennan's poems were not among them. All other attempts to trace these verses have equally failed.

11. Rossetti, *Reminiscences,* p. 170.

12. Obituary, *The Scotsman,* p. 4.

13. W. M. Rossetti, ed., *Ruskin: Rossetti: Preraphaelitism* (London: George Allen, 1899), pp. 129–31. If McLennan's ideas have not withstood the test of time, there are other aspects of the academic scene which have not changed. McLennan, referring to the professorship for which he had applied, wrote to Rossetti, "Of course you are aware that the competition is between the political friends of the candidates, and not between themselves."

in the same year his article on law was published in the eighth edition of the *Encyclopaedia Britannica*.[14]

He practiced at the Scottish bar until 1870, but he was not a successful advocate;[15] he was a poor speaker, and he fought against the conventions of the legal profession.[16] He was also highly critical of the law itself,[17] and much of his effort seems to have gone into attempts to change the legal system, as is indicated in his active part in the agitation which lead to the Court of Session Act, 1868. In the same year he became secretary of the Scottish Society for the Amendment of the Law.[18] He must have further alienated himself from his professional colleagues by preferring to choose his friends from those with whom he shared a common interest in literary and scientific matters.[19] During his later years in Edinburgh his house became an informal center of the local literary and scientific society, and he was a founder member of the Edinburgh Evening Club.[20]

14. It is not obvious why McLennan, a relative newcomer to legal studies, should have contributed this article. Early recognition of ability? The refusal of more eminent men to contribute? Or perhaps an acquaintance with the editors of the eighth edition? The list of contributors offers no clear guide in answering this question for while it includes such living and dead authorities as James Mill, Macaulay, Robert Malthus, Charles Kingsley, Austen Henry Lazard, and Roget (of *Thesaurus* fame), it also contains many lesser names.

15. Obituary, *The Scotsman*, p. 4.

16. E. B. Tylor, "J. F. McLennan," *The Academy* 20 (2 July 1881): 9–10.

17. For example, see McLennan 1861, p. 187: "It would perhaps be difficult to determine which class of human directory laws has been, on the whole, productive of the greatest amount of human misery." See also his criticisms of law-making and written law in the encyclopedia article (1857, pp. 269–71).

18. *The Scotsman* (24 October 1868), p. 2. This is a report of the first meeting of this Society, so that the *DNB* is wrong when it implies that it was the activities of the Scottish Law Amendment Society, with McLennan as secretary, which led to the passing of the Court of Session Act. The Court of Session Act which became law on 31 July 1868 was *An Act to Amend the Procedure in the Court of Session and the Judicial Arrangements in the Superior Courts of Scotland, and to Make Certain Changes in the Other Courts Thereof.*

19. Obituary, *The Scotsman*, p. 4.

20. *Ibid.* For a further description of this club and its members see

His law practice further suffered because of long absences due to sickness in his family[21] and, according to Tylor, because "in 1865 he published a law-book which had the natural and immediate effect of losing him half his briefs. This was *Primitive Marriage*." [22]

In 1862 McLennan had married Mary Bell, the daughter of John Ramsay McCulloch, the statistician and political economist, by whom he had a daughter, his only child.[23] McLennan, unhappy in his legal career, paid fairly frequent visits to the south of England during the 1860s,[24] and in 1870, after the death of his wife, he moved permanently to London. He was elected member of the Ethnological Society of London on 11 January 1870,[25] and he spoke at one of the society's meetings in April of that year.[26] In the following year, Lord Young, then

J. S. Black and G. W. Chrystal, *William Robertson Smith* (London, 1912).

21. Ibid.

22. Tylor, "McLennan," pp. 9–10. This appears to have been McLennan's assessment as is indicated by the following extract from Rossetti's diary; "Tuesday, 9 April [1867]—Maclennan called. He . . . says that his professional income has not of late been improving, but the contrary; which he attributes partly to some prejudice consequent upon his book on *Primitive Marriage*," (*Rossetti Papers 1862–1870*, a compilation by W. M. Rossetti [London: Sands & Co., 1903], p. 229).

23. *DNB*. McLennan's daughter, Ella, does not appear to have married. In 1918, the year in which she gave the bust of her father to the University of Aberdeen, she was still unmarried and living in London.

24. It was during one of these visits that McLennan, writing from South Park, Reigate, contacted Sir John Lubbock; and one gets the impression that they also met. (See *Avebury Papers*, British Museum ms. 49640, letters from McLennan to Lubbock, dated 12 September, 11 October, and 28 October 1867.)

25. *Journal of the Ethnological Society of London*, n.s. 2 (1870): 96.

26. Ibid., p. 351. After this McLennan's interest in the Society appears to have waned. In 1872 he was asked to evaluate a paper on polygamy submitted for publication in the *Journal* by A. L. Lewis but declined to do so (*Reports on papers submitted to the Journal, 1871–1910*. MS A9 of the Royal Anthropological Institute, London). Pencilled against McLennan's name in the *Register of Members, 1879* (MS A31 of the R. A. I.) is a note that he had gone abroad and had not paid his subscription since 1870. J. W. Burrow expresses surprise at the absence of McLennan's name from the membership list of the Anthropological Society but, given McLennan's literary and scientific interests, the company of the Anthropological Society would hardly have suited him (J. W.

Lord Advocate, obtained him the post of parliamentary draftsman for Scotland.[27] He had already taken up this appointment
by July 1871 when Lewis Henry Morgan met him in London,
but was still unhappy and was hoping to get a professorship at
Cambridge so that he could give all of his time to his studies.
He also indicated to Morgan that he would be willing to go
to America if a good job were offered to him.[28] Nothing, however, came of his hopes for an academic life, and the highest
academic recognitions he received were his election as Fellow
of the Royal Society of Edinburgh in 1867 and an honorary
doctorate of law from Aberdeen University in 1874.[29]

McLennan continued in his post as parliamentary draftsman
until 1875 when with a change of government he resigned.[30]
In the same year he married his second wife, Eleonora Anne,
the daughter of Francis Holle Brandram.[31] However, by this
time his conscientious attention to his duties had broken his

Burrow, "Evolution and Anthropology in the 1860's," *Victorian Studies*
7 [1963]: 153).

27. Tylor, "McLennan," pp. 9–10. McLennan was fairly well acquainted with Lord Young, for he offered to arrange for Sir John Lubbock to stay with him during a visit to Scotland (*Avebury Papers,* British
Museum ms. 49641, letter from McLennan to Lubbock, dated 5 October
1869). However, only three months later, McLennan wrote to Lubbock
asking him to influence Gladstone and help him obtain the post of
Queen's Remembrancer because his competitor for the office had the
support of Lord Young. This letter, the last existing one to have passed
between these two men, must have been a very difficult one for a proud
man to write; and McLennan, clearly embarrassed, makes great effort
to justify his request (*Avebury Papers,* British Museum ms. 49641, letter
from McLennan to Lubbock, dated 6 January 1870).

28. L. A. White, ed., "Extracts from the European Travel Journal of
Lewis H. Morgan," *Rochester Historical Society Publications,* vol. 16
(1937). Pages 367–79 cover all the references to McLennan.

29. Tylor wrote of McLennan as being "too erratic to run along the
academic groove far enough to reach its greater honours" (Tylor,
"McLennan," pp. 9–10).

30. Tylor, "McLennan," pp. 9–10. The new government of which
McLennan did not approve was the 1874 Tory Government of Disraeli.
McLennan was a Liberal; in his letter to Lubbock in which he is solicit-
ing support for the obtainment of an appointment (see n. 27 above),
one of the reasons he gives for deserving Gladstone's patronage is the
work he had done for the Liberal cause both as a journalist and barrister.

31. *DNB.*

health, and he never recovered it.[32] For much of the time between 1875 and 1881 McLennan was sick; he suffered from consumption and while wintering in Algiers caught malaria fever.[33] In March 1881 McLennan wrote to Tylor saying that "after being engaged in a grim fight for life for upward of two years" he was getting better and hoped to restart work.[34] He died unexpectedly at his home (Hawthorndene, Hayes Common, Kent) on 16 June 1881.[35]

The bare outlines of McLennan's life are enough to reveal him as a man unable to come to terms with the conventions of the society in which he lived. His failure to achieve success in his legal career and to obtain an academic post may have been a result of his character; certainly his obituaries do not hide the fact that he was the object of very strong emotions. It is worth quoting some passages from these reports.

> His character was very marked and very charming. What lay at the bottom of it was a warm heart and a strong moral feeling, which attached itself most of all to the necessity of truth and hard work. On the surface he was occasionally aggressive and denunciatory, and people who did not know him, or were incapable of appreciating him, were apt to think him disagreeable; especially as he had no respect whatever for persons. But in reality these surface asperities arose entirely from simple earnestness and a somewhat dangerous habit of saying precisely what he thought in the strongest language which occurred to him at the time. [But he was also] exceedingly kind and sensitive in his nature.[36]

Tylor drew a similar distinction between McLennan's acerbity and his kindness,[37] and the writer of his obituary in

32. "M'Lennan," *Encyclopaedia Britannica*, 9th ed. 15:162–63. The author was probably William Robertson Smith who was one of the editors of the ninth edition.

33. Obituary, *The Scotsman*, p. 4.

34. Tylor, "McLennan," pp. 9–10.

35. *DNB*. He probably moved to this address after his second marriage. His earlier London address was 61, Bedford Gardens, Campden Hill.

36. Obituary, *The Scotsman*, p. 4.

37. Tylor, "McLennan," pp. 9–10.

The Athenaeum described him as a "kind and charming companion." [38] In the ninth edition of the *Encyclopaedia Britannica* it is written of him that "in private life M'Lennan was distinguished by his remarkable powers of conversation, by an uncompromising sense of duty, especially of duty to truth, by a warm and affectionate disposition, and by his readiness to help all workers in science, especially young men of promise." [39]

Because these remarks about the basic agreeableness of McLennan are in contradiction to received ideas about him, and could be dismissed as the inevitable and conventional eulogisms of the obituary, it is extremely valuable that we have some contemporaneous descriptions of McLennan. First, there are the reminiscences of William Michael Rossetti, who met McLennan a number of times and remembered him as being "of the unorthodox turn in matters of faith and speculation. . . . His mind was rapid in its processes and full of acuteness; his speech had discernment and point. He was among the men whose society I should have best liked to cultivate. . . ." [40]

Another account of McLennan is to be found in the diaries of none other than L. H. Morgan. McLennan appears to have gone out of his way to be helpful to Morgan, whom he first met in London on 5 July 1871. Morgan was cordially received and wrote of McLennan: "I like him quite well." [41] McLennan offered to arrange a dinner for him together with Herbert Spencer and Sir John Lubbock, but neither of these men was available, and Morgan dined alone with McLennan on 6 July. [42] They appear to have met several times after that, for on 27 July Morgan wrote, "My friend McLennan, for I think I may now call him such, breakfasted with us yesterday morning, and we had a good time." [43] On 27 July McLennan took Morgan to the Athenaeum to introduce him to Sir Henry Maine, and on the following day obtained for Morgan an order for ad-

38. *The Athenaeum* (London, 25 June 1881), p. 851.
39. "M'Lennan," *Britannica*, 9th ed., pp. 162–63.
40. Rossetti, *Reminiscences*, p. 170.
41. White, "Morgan," p. 368.
42. Ibid.
43. Ibid., p. 371.

mission to the House of Lords.[44] Morgan for his part tried to help his new friend, and having learned that McLennan would like an academic appointment and would be willing to go to America wrote to President White of Cornell University urging him to make McLennan an offer.[45] Furthermore, when he met Maine he told him that he and Lubbock should unite to procure McLennan a post at Cambridge.[46] Morgan had a high opinion of McLennan's ability and wrote of the enthusiasm which McLennan had for his studies.[47] However, perhaps there was some strain in their friendship, since when Morgan directed his publishers to send copies of *Systems of Consanguinity and Affinity of the Human Family* to various people (including Huxley, Spencer, and Darwin), McLennan's name was not included on the list.[48]

This meeting of McLennan and Morgan took place before the start of their bitter argument over the validity of their respective evolutionary frameworks, the nature of relationship terminologies, and the true meaning of exogamy and endogamy. However, Morgan appears to have had a similar character to McLennan,[49] and Tylor remarked that "probably neither combatant was much hurt." [50]

It is a feature of all McLennan's writing from 1865, the year of publication of *Primitive Marriage* onwards, that it is con-

44. Ibid., pp. 374–75.
45. Ibid., p. 368.
46. Ibid., p. 375.
47. Ibid., p. 368.
48. Ibid., p. 371.
49. *Cf.* B. J. Stern, *Lewis Henry Morgan: Social Evolutionist* (University of Chicago Press, 1931); and C. Resek, *Lewis Henry Morgan: American Scholar* (University of Chicago Press, 1960). Sir Henry Maine had the same view of McLennan and Morgan. In 1878 he wrote to Tylor complaining about what a curious man Morgan was and likening him to McLennan (a letter dated 27 May 1878, which was found inside Tylor's copy of Morgan's *Ancient Society* in the Institute of Social Anthropology, University of Oxford, and subsequently published in *Man* 51 [July 1951]: 104). A few years later Maine wrote to Morgan saying that McLennan's "illness has much increased his acerbity of temper" and that he was working on a book "which is to annihilate all his adversaries including myself." (Quoted by B. J. Stern [1931], p. 144).
50. Tylor, "McLennan," pp. 9–10.

cerned with either the provision of additional evidence for his original hypothesis or the defense of his hypothesis from the slightest modification. There is no doubt that McLennan was a very polemical writer and that he became a more aggressive disputant as he grew older so that he ended his life a virtual paranoiac.[51] It is worth examining McLennan's works in their chronological order since they give a good insight into the development of his thoughts.

II

McLennan's earliest published articles were presumably written no later than 1853 (although there may have been some before this), when he was doing literary work in London. A collection of Pre-Raphaelite verse which McLennan wrote and to which Rossetti makes brief reference belongs to this earlier period and can be dated as pre-1855.[52] The first serious and attributable article is that on law written for the eighth edition of the *Encyclopaedia Britannica*.[53] This article is a valuable document in tracing the development of McLennan's ideas, especially when it is compared with *Primitive Marriage*, which was published eight years later; I shall return to this point below.

Between 1857 and 1865 five further works came from McLennan's pen. Of these, two appeared in 1860, a popular magazine article and a pamphlet on Scottish art and artists of the period,[54] and a further two were concerned with legal matters.[55] The fifth, a review article on a number of works dealing with India, is the most important of his publications from this

51. Maine's letter to Tylor (see n. 49 above) closes with the remark, "McLennan . . . lives in fear lest anybody should get scent of his supposed discoveries.

52. See n. 10 above.

53. McLennan (1857).

54. McLennan (1860a and 1860b). Rossetti attributes the work on *Scottish Art and Artists* to the joint authorship of McLennan and Alexander Smith, the poet (*Reminiscences*, p. 170). In the *British Museum Catalogue of Printed Books*, the pseudonym, Iconoclast, under which this pamphlet was published, is identified as J. C. MacLennan.

55. McLennan (1861 and 1864).

period, particularly for the assessment of the development of his anthropological ideas.[56]

Following the publication of *Primitive Marriage* in 1865 there appeared an article in *Argosy*, entitled "Bride-Catching" and consisting of the examples of marriage by capture taken from *Primitive Marriage* together with some additional cases.[57] McLennan later considered substituting this article for chapter 2 of *Primitive Marriage* in the first edition of *Studies in Ancient History*,[58] but did not do so. In the same year (1866) he also published an article on "Kinship in Ancient Greece,"[59] which was a test of the hypothesis contained in *Primitive Marriage* by the use of ancient Greek material and "was undertaken on a challenge from Mr. Gladstone, who believed that the scheme was inconsistent with Homeric facts."[60] It is in a footnote to this article that McLennan first saw the potential importance of totemism as a stage through which all societies have passed in their evolution.[61]

McLennan's third publication in 1866 is also worth drawing attention to; it is a piece entitled "Concerning Easy-writing" which appeared in the *Argosy*.[62] His name is listed as being the author both in the contents of the relevant volume and beneath the title on the article's first page. However, at the end of the piece there is the italicized signature—Jonathan Jones. The article appears to be a parody of a journalist or a journalistic style of the time, but it has not been possible to discover any further information.

The following year (1867) McLennan published another major work, also unrelated to his anthropological studies. This was *Memoir of Thomas Drummond, R.E., F.R.A.S., Under*

56. McLennan (1863). One of the books reviewed in this article is William McCulloch's *Account of the Valley of Munnipore and of the Hill Tribes*. This McCulloch was McLennan's brother-in-law.

57. McLennan (1866d).

58. McLennan (1876), p. vi.

59. McLennan (1866b and 1866c).

60. McLennan (1876), p. vii.

61. McLennan (1866b), p. 588, n. 1.

62. McLennan (1866a).

Secretary to the Lord Lieutenant of Ireland, 1835–1840.[63] This is a straightforward biography of a dutiful but uninspiring public servant,[64] and the only interesting piece of information which one can glean from it is that McLennan and Harriet Martineau were acquaintances, which merely confirms the picture of McLennan moving in literary circles.[65]

McLennan returned to the mainstream of his interests with an article on totem in the first edition of *Chamber's Encyclopaedia.*[66] This is a brief piece, and together with a review article of James Fergusson's *Tree and Serpent Worship*[67] they represent forerunners to his articles "The Worship of Animals and Plants" published in 1869 and 1870.[68] These articles are among the most influential that McLennan ever wrote although his intention was simply to reinforce the scheme of social evolution mapped out in *Primitive Marriage.* In 1869 McLennan also published an article "The Early History of Man" [69] in which he considers two burning questions of the time—the antiquity of man and whether man had advanced from a state of barbarism or had sunk from a higher level of civilization. This paper also includes a discussion of the method of the study of ancient history by means of existing but symbolic forms of old practices.

During his years as parliamentary draftsman McLennan published nothing, but after his retirement the first edition of *Studies in Ancient History* appeared in 1876. This book is composed of a number of different essays, some republications of old articles and other original pieces. The two works already

63. McLennan (1867).
64. It would appear that McLennan had written this *Memoir* at the request of Drummond's sister. This information was provided by Mr. J. H. Andrews of Trinity College, Dublin, and is to be found among the Larcom Papers in the National Library, Dublin. The relevant document is a letter dated 8 August 1865 from McLennan to Thomas Larcom, then Under-Secretary.
65. McLennan (1867), p. v.
66. McLennan (1868). Although this article is not signed, J. F. McLennan's name appears among the list of contributors, and he later admitted authorship (see McLennan [1876], p. vii).
67. McLennan (1869a).
68. McLennan (1869c, 1869d, and 1870).
69. McLennan (1869b).

noticed which are reprinted in this book are *Primitive Marriage* in its entirety and "Kinship in Ancient Greece." The four new pieces are all criticisms of then recently published works on the topic of social evolution. There is a long essay entitled "The Classificatory System of Relationships," which deals with Morgan's *Systems*.[70] Then there is briefer comment on Bachofen's *Das Mutterrecht*,[71] a piece entitled "Communal Marriage" which treats of Lubbock's *Origin of Civilisation*,[72] and another called "Divisions of the Ancient Irish Family" which is a refutation of Maine's *Lectures on the Early History of Institutions*.[73]

Although McLennan's next original paper "The Levirate and Polyandry" [74] is an attempt to provide further evidence for the original hypothesis by demonstrating that the existence of the levirate is a survival which indicates the previous existence of polyandry—a vital stage in his evolutionary scheme—he does not miss the opportunity to criticize further the ideas of Spencer and Lubbock with regard to the development of marriage. The next month, also in *The Fortnightly Review*, he wrote an explanatory paper "Exogamy and Endogamy," [75] words which he had invented and which he claimed no one understood. The paper is mainly concerned with correcting Herbert Spencer's "misuse" of the terms, but the argument went little further for after "a short rejoinder" Spencer withdrew, complaining that "Mr. McLennan has . . . introduced into his rejoinder a tone which renders it undesirable to continue the discussion." [76]

70. L. H. Morgan, *Systems of Consanguinity and Affinity of the Human Family*. Smithsonian Contributions to Knowledge, no. 218 (Washington, D. C., 1871)

71. J. J. Bachofen, *Das Mutterrecht* (Stuttgart, 1861).

72. Sir John Lubbock, *The Origin of Civilisation and the Primitive Condition of Man* (London, 1870).

73. H. S. Maine, *Lectures on the Early History of Institutions* (London, 1875). McLennan had intended an article on this subject some time before Maine's work was published, and as early as 16 November 1866 McLennan had written to Thomas Larcom saying how glad he would be when Drummond's *Memoir* was finished so that he could begin a study of the ancient Irish (see Larcom Papers).

74. McLennan (1877a).

75. McLennan (1877b).

76. Herbert Spencer, "A Short Rejoinder," *The Fortnightly Review* n.s., 21 (1 June 1877): 902.

This was the last original paper that McLennan published in his lifetime.[77]

Four years after his death, in 1885, appeared *The Patriarchal Theory* on which both McLennan and his youngest brother Donald had been working at the time of the former's death.[78] Donald McLennan went on to complete his brother's work, basing it on the papers which he had left. The idea of this book came to McLennan in 1879, and it was planned as the destruction of the patriarchal theory—that is to say, the generally and popularly held notion that the patriarchal family was the primordial social unit. McLennan regarded it as essential to destroy this erroneous belief before offering the public an alternative theory. Since at that time the main upholder of the patriarchal theory (and an extremely widely read and influential one at that) was Sir Henry Maine, this book is in effect an admitted polemic directed at his ideas.[79]

In the following year, 1886, appeared a second edition of *Studies in Ancient History*,[80] the contents of which are basically the same as those of the first edition but with the addition of a preface by Donald McLennan, which is mainly given up to explaining the meanings given by McLennan to the terms exogamy and endogamy, the inclusion of more examples of marriage by capture (taken from the *Argosy* article),[81] and various editorial notes. Two years later Donald McLennan completed and published his brother's article on the origin of

77. Carl Resek claims that a review of Morgan's *Ancient Society* which appeared in *The Athenaeum* on 29 December 1877 was the work of McLennan (*Morgan,* p. 143, n. 18). Although I have no definite evidence with which to contradict this opinion the review certainly does not read as if it were by McLennan, since the reviewer concentrates on such aspects as the antiquity of man, and the argument of degradation versus development of human society. Although McLennan had written on these topics (cf. McLennan, 1869b), they are not those which one might have expected McLennan to single out for discussion considering that *Ancient Society* contains a long note specifically denying the correctness of McLennan's ideas.
78. McLennan (1885), p. xi.
79. Ibid., p. x.
80. McLennan (1886).
81. McLennan (1866c).

exogamy,[82] an outline sketch of which had been written in great haste in the spring of 1877 [83] and which had presumably been intended as part of McLennan's dispute with Spencer on this topic.

Then fifteen years after his death appeared his lifetime's work, *Studies in Ancient History, The Second Series*.[84] This is the work for which *The Patriarchal Theory* was intended to clear the way.[85] Although McLennan may have planned this as his major work, it is unfair to judge him by it considering the delay in its publication and the vicissitudes it suffered prior to its appearance. Indeed it is a miracle that the book ever appeared at all, and it stands as a monument less to McLennan's genius than to the loyalty of his brother, his wife, and his friends. Donald McLennan died while the work was still in preparation, and his place was taken by William Robertson Smith until 1894 when he himself died. The book was completed by McLennan's widow and Arthur Platt, but even the former did not survive to see it in print.[86] The work is divided into two parts; the first consists of a number of rather disparate essays on the methods, techniques, problems and findings in the study of ancient history. The second is composed of a mass of ethnographic material sorted into regions. The underlying message is still McLennan's original one—that the path to civilization lies through a stage of matriliny. By 1896 the work was almost an anachronism, and those parts of his argument which had survived the test of time and criticism had already been presented in far more cogent form by other writers.

McLennan's literary output was not great; and considering that it was stretched over forty years (if his posthumous publications are included) and that many items were published twice or even more times, it is small. Furthermore his anthropological interest was astonishingly narrow, almost obsessively so when one compares it both in volume and range with that

82. McLennan (1888).
83. Ibid., p. 94.
84. McLennan (1896).
85. McLennan (1896), p. v.
86. Ibid., p. vi and p. ix.

of a man like Wake.[87] Indeed the comparison with Wake is
very instructive since both belonged to the legal profession
and their anthropological studies were little more than hobbies,
and both came from provincial and middle-class backgrounds.[88]
Here, however, the similarity ends for while Wake has been
forgotten for over half a century, even today few textbooks
fail to refer to McLennan and even a number of more special-
ized books still bestow upon him more than a passing glance.[89]
McLennan's name has survived not because he was right (he
was not), nor because he had a circle of influential friends, but
probably because of his sheer tenacity in the promulgation of
what was, for him, a single idea. It is not particularly relevant
that this idea was also wrong; what is important is that it was
of a radical enough nature to make others stop and think and
that McLennan did not allow it to be forgotten.

It is now time to turn and consider the basis of this idea, the
the evolutionary scheme as presented in *Primitive Marriage*.

III

The argument in *Primitive Marriage* is easy to follow. Its
simplicity arises in part from the expository method of its author; for even if McLennan was a poor lawyer, one can see in
his work an incisive legal mind being brought to bear on the
problems.

In the first place the book is presented as an essay in scientific
history for philosophers, and as a novelty for the public.[90] This

87. C. S. Wake, *The Development of Marriage and Kinship*, ed. R.
Needham (University of Chicago Press, 1967, 1st ed., London, 1889).
See Wake's bibliography in the Editor's Introduction, pp. xliii–xlvii.
However, one must not overlook the versatility of McLennan, who pub-
lished on several topics and in several literary forms.

88. Ibid. See Editor's Introduction for a discussion of his life and
work.

89. See, for example, C. Lévi-Strauss, *Totemism*, trans. R. Needham
(Boston, 1963), and *The Elementary Structures of Kinship*, ed. R. Needham (Boston, 1969); John Beattie, *Other Cultures* (New York, 1964);
Godfrey Lienhardt, *Social Anthropology* (Oxford Paperbacks, 1966);
and Robin Fox, *Kinship and Marriage* (Pelican, 1967).

90. McLennan, *Primitive Marriage* (hereafter cited as *PM*), this
volume, p. 3.

is, perhaps, why the stress is first placed on marriage by capture and that only then is it conceded that it may have bearing on a number of other unsolved sociological problems. The first chapter is concerned with an explanation and justification of the method employed. This is to the effect that the study of the most primitive peoples will demonstrate the nature of earliest society and that a symbolic action is evidence of the previous existence of an equivalent but actual practice;[91] the validity of these assumptions being assured by argument rather than by evidence. In the second chapter the form of marriage by capture, that is to say the legal symbol of a former practice, is introduced.[92] McLennan rejects the existing theories which explain marriage by capture through girlish prudery and lists examples of the form of marriage by capture—that is, those cases where the capture is ceremonial or ritual since the two parties to the wedding have already agreed upon it. The third chapter goes on to consider what the origin of such a ceremony may have been, and the conclusion reached is that "it must have been *the system* of certain tribes to capture women . . . for wives." [93] This answer shifts the question to how real marriage by capture may have originated. The argument then follows these lines: marriage by capture could not have originated in a tribe where marriage was prohibited outside the tribe— that is, in an endogamous group (using McLennan's meaning). Accordingly it must have developed among exogamous groups, and this argument includes the explicit assumption that among primitive peoples there are no friendly relationships between different tribes. The position of the argument at the end of the chapter is that exogamy as tribal law, hostility between tribes, and marriage by capture are all closely interrelated; and finally, where the form but not the practice now exists, then this tribe must have been exogamous in the past. The next three chapters (4, 5, and 6) are concerned with the proof of this: first, the evidence that among some peoples wives are taken by capture;

91. McLennan's "symbols" are the same as Tylor's "survivals."
92. "Marriage by capture" is the taking of women by force so that they may become the wives of their abductors.
93. *PM*, p. 20.

second, that where such a trait exists it is coincidental with exogamy; and finally, that war is the normal relationship among primitive groups. The titles of the three chapters indicate the progress of the argument. Having to his satisfaction proved these points, McLennan is able to conclude that "wherever capture, or the form of capture, prevails, or has prevailed, there prevails, or has prevailed, exogamy." [94] He further claims that the converse will be true—that the existence of exogamy indicates at least traces of marriage by capture and that existing evidence suggests that the system of capturing wives is a stage through which every society has passed.

The question now becomes—what is the origin of exogamy or marriage by capture? McLennan's answer is female infanticide, which besides forcing men to find wives outside their group would also give rise to polyandry. He then goes on to suggest various ways in which primitive peoples may be classified according to their marriage customs. He identifies five types of marriage as different forms of pure exogamy and two as forms of pure endogamy; and although he notes that there is a progression in this classification, the actual ranking depends on whether exogamy is older than endogamy or vice versa; this decision he postpones to a later point.

McLennan has now arrived at what he considers to be the most important part of his work,[95] and he lays out the propositions which he intends to develop. Of these propositions it is the first which is the most famous and the one which has had the greatest influence. It is "that the most ancient system in which the idea of blood-relationship was embodied, was the system of kinship through females only." [96] Thus in chapter 8 he sets out his stages of social evolution. The earliest social existence that McLennan posits consists of groups in which men are held together by companionship and in which the ties of kinship are not recognized. The next stage is that of kinship through females only for the reason that the tie with the mother

94. *PM*, p. 57.
95. *PM*, p. 3. "I think that the most important portions of my work are Chapters 8 and 9. . . ."
96. *PM*, p. 61.

is likely to be recognized before, and be more certain than, that with the father. Within the matrilineal horde, the child's tie is more with the horde than with the mother, and the men hold the women in common. This period of general promiscuity gave way to one in which promiscuity is regulated, to a stage of polyandry. McLennan provides evidence for the almost universal distribution of polyandry of which he recognizes two forms. The "ruder" form is that in which the various husbands of a woman are unrelated, and the "less rude," that in which the husbands are brothers. The former McLennan named Nair polyandry, and the latter Tibetan. Nair polyandry is associated with matriliny; and Tibetan polyandry, which presumes patrilocal residence, marks the beginnings of patrilineal descent. When Tibetan polyandry passed away it left a trace of itself in the obligation of the younger brother to marry his elder brother's widow. Thus while the levirate and widow inheritance are relics of the former state of polyandry, polyandrous unions are in turn evidence of a former rule of matriliny. Furthermore, since McLennan argues that both exogamy and polyandry are the result of the same cause—that is, a shortage of women—all exogamous races must also have been polyandrous.

The next step is to indicate that the earliest groups were homogeneous, since before the recognition of kinship through women the children of the captured wives would merely be regarded as belonging to the group. With the recognition of female kinship the group became heterogeneous since the children of the captured women would then be regarded as belonging to different "stocks." [97] The presence of different stocks within a single horde made marriage within the horde possible and consistent with the law of exogamy; and because the different parts of the horde were not hostile to each other, the system of marriage without capture came into existence. The recognition of kinship through females would affiliate the children to the mother rather than to the group, and this would give rise to the formation of families, a development which

97. For McLennan's argument the conception of common stock results from the recognition of blood ties. See *PM*, p. 63.

would be helped by the adoption of separate residences. This is the origin of the Nair polyandric family, and the development from this is to the adelphic Tibetan form with kinship through males. The result of patrilineal-patrilocal groups was the reappearance of homogeneous groups and with them the need for exogamous marriage; the return of which, McLennan assumes, will again be accompanied by marriage by capture.

McLennan also proposes an alternative form of evolution; the exogamous group which has grown heterogeneous through the recognition of kinship through females can intermarry within itself without breaking the rule of exogamy. The superiority which the group assumes as a result of their independence from other groups in matters of women will result in the prohibition of marriage with these inferior groups and a caste will be formed. With the development of male kinship within the caste, the various kindreds of which it is composed assume a fictional common ancestry so that the caste becomes an endogamous tribe. This lengthy chapter closes with some comments on the blood feud, which McLennan sees as being incompatible with a matrilineal exogamous people and its suppression among such people resulting in a reduction in the incidence of infanticide. In patrilineal societies, however, the blood feud is directly responsible for the perpetuation of infanticide and exogamy.

In chapter 9 McLennan is concerned with demonstrating the breakdown of exogamy in advancing communities, but in a way which did not result in endogamy. The argument in this chapter is perhaps less clear than in the earlier ones, and this is partly because much of it is directed against the Patriarchal Theory that social evolution began with the family and developed into the state, with adoption as a mechanism in this growth. McLennan, as has been indicated above, proposed a reverse course of social evolution, the horde being the earliest social grouping and the individual family the highest and most recent development. Exogamy declined at the same rate as the family grew, and this process was, in turn, coupled with an increase in property rights.

No doubt the ideas and argument contained in *Primitive*

Marriage do not appear very startling to the modern reader; but in its time—a period in which the dominance of men and the subordinacy of women went unquestioned—the suggestion that, during the evolution of society, these roles were reversed was indeed revolutionary, and it is worth considering how Mc-Lennan may have developed such an unorthodox notion.

IV

The link between McLennan's method and that of the Scottish philosophers of the preceding century has been a matter of some doubt and question. If one can regard these Scottish philosophers as being among the forefathers of social anthropology then there is a hiatus between the decline of their influence and the appearance of *Primitive Marriage,* a pause which in England was filled with the rise and decline of utilitarianism. J. W. Burrow has suggested that the important thing about McLennan may be his nationality and that he is a direct descendant of the Scottish school. Although he regards this idea as an attractive one he sees a major drawback to accepting it;[98] namely to account for the undoubted change in McLennan's ideas and method between 1857, the date of the encyclopedia article on law, and 1865, which marked the appearance of *Primitive Marriage.* I shall return to this problem below, but first it is important to indicate certain features of McLennan's education and life which would support the idea of him as a direct descendant of the Scottish school.

In 1837, and there is no evidence of any change by 1845, the syllabus for the M.A. degree at King's College, Aberdeen, included Dugald Stewart's moral philosophy;[99] so that at least in one aspect, McLennan was educated in the tradition of the Scottish school. There is no particular evidence that McLennan was ever much exposed to the teachings of utilitarianism, while if his London acquaintances introduced him to Comtism (as would almost certainly have been the case) he gives no sign of having been influenced by it. Furthermore, during the period

98. J. W. Burrow, *Evolution and Society* (Cambridge University Press, 1966), p. 233.
99. P. J. Anderson, *The Arts Curriculum* (Aberdeen, 1892), p. 17.

when he is reputed to have been writing for *The Leader* there is a review article entitled "Scottish Metaphysics, Past and Present" which concludes with the sentence "Scottish metaphysics are not and never have been dead." [100] While there is no evidence that McLennan is the author of this piece, it is not beyond the bounds of possibility but is within those of probability. Finally, one cannot fail to note the similiarity between Sydney Smith's comment on the Scottish historians who begin every subject "a few days before the flood, and come *gradually* down to the reign of George the third," [101] and a critic's remark about the *Memoir of Thomas Drummond* that "Mr. M'Lennan has thought it requisite to write a complete history of Ireland, from the Danaans to Drummond." [102]

All this is admittedly speculative except for the fact that McLennan was undoubtedly introduced to the tradition of the Scottish school and that his works show an application of its method. It is a pity that McLennan himself was not more explicit about the influences which were at work on him. In *Primitive Marriage* he refers to Aristotle, Maine, Montesquieu, and Dugald Stewart, but otherwise his bibliography consists entirely of ethnographies. He is only slightly more explicit in his later works, from which one can derive the information that he had not read Bachofen's *Das Mutterrecht* (1861) when preparing *Primitive Marriage*[103] and that he did not discover Millar's *Origin of Ranks* (1779) until 1871.[104] There is no evidence that he was greatly influenced by *The Origin of Species* and there is no mention of it in any of his works. He had, however, corresponded with Darwin in 1874 and before about the stages of social evolution,[105] and in the preface to *Studies in Ancient History* he notes the existence of *The De-*

100. *The Leader* (London, 11 November 1854).
101. C. W. New, *The Life of Henry Brougham to 1830* (Oxford University Press, 1961), p. 223.
102. Anonymous review of *Memoir of Thomas Drummond*, in *The Athenaeum*, no. 2087 (24 August 1867): 234–5. The review continues "a more arid, dead level and good-for-nothing tract we never had the misfortune to meet.
103. McLennan (1866b), p. 582.
104. McLennan (1876), p. 420.
105. McLennan (1896), pp. 50–55.

scent of Man but postpones consideration until a later date.[106] In fact, he never returned to do so, and Hale later suggested that McLennan modified his views on the earliest social condition of man to fit with Darwin's ideas.[107] At one place McLennan refers to the work of Giraud-Teulon, a pupil of Bachofen, but can find nothing in it to criticize.[108]

Nor is there much internal evidence in *Primitive Marriage* which can give a guide to the roots of his ideas. His work, by the standards of the period, is remarkably free from analogies and metaphors borrowed from other disciplines. There are references to the limitations of geology and philology as sources of information about the origin and early progress of civilization,[109] some simple geological metaphors,[110] and a botanical one which appears to have given him the idea of exogamy and endogamy.[111]

None of this is particularly helpful; but before accepting McLennan's ideas as a reflection of his nationality, it is necessary to return and consider the one major drawback to this conclusion which Burrow has posited. This is to account for the undeniable change in McLennan's presentation of much of

106. McLennan (1876), pp. ix–x.

107. H. Hale, review of J. F. McLennan's *Studies in Ancient History,* in *Science* 8 (17 December 1886): 569–70. The basis for Hale writing this is McLennan's criticism of Lubbock's earliest stage of civilization, that of communal marriage. Originally McLennan himself had proposed a very similar condition (cf. *PM*, p. 69 *et seq.*). Darwin, in *The Descent of Man,* noted that among the higher anthropoids there was little promiscuous sexual intercourse and accordingly this could hardly have been a condition of the earliest human societies. He does not deny the existence of undue licentiousness among savages but regards this as a decline into depravity (C. Darwin, *The Descent of Man* [New York, 1874], pp. 672–73).

108. McLennan (1876), p. x; A. Giraud-Teulon, *Les Origines de la Famille* (Geneva, 1874). Although a pupil of Bachofen, Giraud-Teulon later became a follower of Durkheim (see his article "Sur les origines de la famille," *Bulletin de la Société d'Anthropologie de Lyon* 27 [1902]: 34–46). It is an interesting commentary on Durkheim's ideas on the family that Giraud-Teulon was able to accept them without having to modify greatly his own original ideas.

109. *PM*, p. 5.

110. *PM*, p. 19.

111. *PM*, p. 22 n.

the same material between 1857 and 1865. It was in the course of his researches for the encyclopedia article on law that McLennan unearthed the material that was to form the basis of *Primitive Marriage,* but there is no sign in the earlier work of the use to which it was to be put later. Furthermore, in the law article McLennan refers to the ideas of such thinkers as Hooker, J. S. Mill, Whewell, Comte, and Mackintosh to whom he never refers in his later works. It is unlikely that McLennan had already worked out the ideas presented in *Primitive Marriage* by the time he wrote the encyclopedia article. Even if he had, such an article would not have been the place to present such radical views (it is doubtful if they would have been accepted by the editors), especially since at that time McLennan had been a law student for only a few years. An encyclopedia article is not usually a place for original thought but rather for received ideas. The fact that McLennan refers in this article to a number of writers who exert no influence in his later works would seem to confirm this view; accordingly the article is not helpful in trying to trace the development of McLennan's thought.

While there is no evidence of the schema which was in due course to form the basis of his evolutionary stages, one can in the encyclopedia article see the focusing of McLennan's interest on certain topics. He claims that the origins of law are to be seen in the descriptions of early societies and he labels marriage together with personal safety, property, and government as one of the fundamental social institutions. Indeed he goes so far as to write that "laws may be said to have first grown round the marriage relation, next round the institution of property." [112]

However, there is one passage in particular which stresses the change in McLennan's argument, since it appears in both works but for opposing purposes. In the encyclopedia article he wrote,

> Society obviously commences in the family; the society
> of parents into which every human being is born, and
> in which are to be found the germs of that subordination

112. McLennan (1857), p. 256.

J. F. Mc Lennan.

Photograph courtesy the Master and Fellows of Trinity College, Cambridge; signature courtesy the British Museum.

1

Photograph courtesy the Master and Fellows of Trinity College,
Cambridge; signature courtesy the British Museum.

to, and recognition of authority which are essential to the civil state; the state where the government is patriarchal is indeed the prolongation of the family. As the banyan tends to surround itself with a forest of its own offshoots, so the family tends to multiply families around it, till it becomes the centre of a tribe.[113]

This statement should be directly compared with several passages in *Primitive Marriage*; perhaps the most striking being,

> The old theory of the composition of States, was based upon the tendency of families to multiply round a central family, whose head represented the original progenitor of them all. The family, under the government of a father, was assumed to be the primary group—the elementary social unit; in it were found at once the germs of the State, and of sovereign authority. Many circumstances recommended this theory, and none more than its apparent simplicity. It was easy to find abundant analogies for the prolongation of the family into the State. A family tends to multiply families around it, till it becomes the centre of a tribe, just as the banyan tends to surround itself with a forest of its own offshoots. . . .
>
> The origin of the State on this view is so simple, that a child may comprehend it. But it is very easily shown that the theory cannot be supported.[114]

Or again, more briefly,

> The order of social development, in our view, is then, that the tribe stands first; the gens or house next; and last of all, the family.[115]

The question whether or not McLennan, at the time he wrote the encyclopedia article, had already formed the ideas which later appeared in *Primitive Marriage* has been raised above. There is one piece of evidence which clearly indicates that he had not. This is his article, published anonymously in 1863, "Hill Tribes in India" in which there is still no sign of

113. Ibid., pp. 255–56.
114. *PM*, pp. 106–7.
115. *PM*, p. 111.

the ideas which were to emerge in *Primitive Marriage* only two years later. Indeed in this article McLennan was able to write that female infanticide, soon to become a vital mechanism in his evolutionary scheme, must result from superstition[116] and that marriage by capture was practiced only by the rudest societies, and even among them was the exception rather than the rule.[117] Furthermore, although there are evolutionary undertones in his article, McLennan is as much concerned with explaining cultural differences by means of environmental factors as by social evolution.[118] Thus one can narrow down Burrow's question and ask "what was it that made McLennan turn his ideas on their head between 1863 and 1865?" It could have been the realization that many of his facts did not fit into the conventional scheme, or it could have been an outside agent.

Burrow has pointed to Maine's *Ancient Law* (1861) as the influence which revolutionized McLennan's view;[119] and since we do not know the date at which McLennan read *Ancient Law,* there are no grounds for rejecting the suggestion, which has proved well worth pursuing. Maine in *Ancient Law* follows very closely the conventional approach and assumes the patriarchal family to be the origin of the state. However, what Maine was setting out to do was to put jurisprudence on a scientific footing, which basically was to explain the development of law, something which earlier jurisprudents, so Maine claimed, had, with the exception of Montesquieu, failed to do.[120] Although he later tried to deny it, there are indications in *Ancient Law* that Maine thought he was dealing with the whole range of primitive societies and that "the primeval condition of the human race" could be accounted for by the Patri-

116. McLennan (1863), p. 408.
117. Ibid., p. 409.
118. Ibid., pp. 418–22. So completely did McLennan's thinking change that he, on re-reading this article in 1867, was shocked by it, and asked Lubbock not to read it nor mention it to anyone else (*Avebury Papers,* British Museum ms. 49640, letter from McLennan to Lubbock, dated 28 October 1867).
119. Burrow, *Evolution,* p. 232.
120. H. S. Maine, *Ancient Law* (Boston, 1963), p. 114.

archal Theory.[121] Maine also had rather narrow views about ethnographic material and about primitive societies, whose form he considered to be identifiable in the early chapters of Genesis.[122]

It is quite noticeable that Maine is the only contemporary theorist to whom McLennan refers in *Primitive Marriage*, and it is more than possible that McLennan on reading *Ancient Law* gathered from it both the idea of placing material in an evolutionary framework and the fact that the conventional patriarchal theory was inadequate to account for the meaning of the ethnographic facts of which he was aware. If this supposition is correct, then there is not much mystery surrounding the creation of the schema presented in *Primitive Marriage*. Given a clever Scottish lawyer, aware of the school of conjectural history (and McLennan regarded *Primitive Marriage* as a history book), who was acquainted with a collection of apparently bizarre customs (including matriliny) and a work on the development of society which could not absorb these facts, and one has all the ingredients required for the appearance of such a work as *Primitive Marriage*.

There may, however, be more to it than this, since Maine plays a central part throughout McLennan's works. Maine is McLennan's chief antagonist; McLennan's argument with Morgan has overshadowed, at least in the minds of anthropologists, the prominence which Maine has in McLennan's writings. McLennan wrote more in refutation of Maine's ideas than of anyone else's. It is not immediately obvious that *Primitive Marriage* is an attack on Maine's position,[123] because the polemic aspect of this early book is more muted. In later works it appears more strongly. McLennan's article "Divisions of the Ancient Irish Family" is a critique of Maine's article on this topic in his *The Early History of Institutions* (1871); the whole of *The Patriarchal Theory* is directed against Maine as the leading expositor of this theory. The preface to *The Patriarchal Theory* contains some revealing remarks which

121. Ibid., p. 118.
122. Ibid., p. 119.
123. But see pp. 48, 94, 103, and 108.

Donald McLennan has to make; for example, "the view expressed in *Primitive Marriage* that Agnation was, at a certain
stage, generally prevalent, in stating which it may be believed
that he yielded somewhat to the authority of Sir Henry
Maine." [124] Again, later in the same preface, Donald McLennan states his brother's position both with reference to the
Patriarchal Theory and to Maine.

> From the time of Plato downwards, theories of human
> society have been current in which the family living
> under the headship of a father is accepted as the ulti-
> mate social unit. These theories have taken various
> shapes, but in his opinion the most important, as well
> as the most influential, shape to be taken account of
> is that represented in the works of Sir Henry Maine. In
> the hands of the more prominent amongst its older ad-
> vocates within the period of modern thought the Patri-
> archal Theory, as it is called, was mainly a theory of the
> source of sovereignty, and in this aspect it had gradually
> ceased to attract attention. With Sir Henry Maine, on
> the other hand, the theory becomes a theory of the
> origin of society, or at least of the earliest stage of society
> in which Comparative Jurisprudence is called upon to
> take interest. And at the same time the theory is ex-
> pressly based on a comparative study of early societies,
> so that it comes into direct conflict with every theory of
> the origin of society which does not accept the family
> as the primitive unit.
>
> It was necessary, therefore, for my brother to take
> notice of this theory, and to do so on the scale which
> the intrinsic importance of the question demanded . . .
> it was felt that the enormous prestige which the Patri-
> archal Theory has gained through Sir Henry Maine's
> advocacy made it impossible to separate the argument
> from the form which he has impressed on it. In English-
> speaking countries, at least, this is the one form in which
> the theory is current, and no discussion of it would have
> been useful which did not closely follow the statements
> of the author of *Ancient Law*, a book which, for more

124. McLennan (1885), p. v, n.

than twenty years, has profoundly influenced the whole teaching of Jurisprudence in our country.[125]

For McLennan, Maine undoubtedly symbolized conventional thinking, but besides his theories Maine was also an ideal representation of everything to which McLennan was either antagonistic or to which he had aspired and had failed to achieve. They offer an odd contrast. Maine was a successful lawyer and academic, part of the establishment, the recipient of a knighthood and many other honors, certainly a conservative and occasionally a Tory, and a man whose ideas received popular acclaim.[126] McLennan came from a humbler background, was a comparative failure as a lawyer, a Liberal, never obtained an academic post, and was accorded only minor academic honors, while his ideas were not popularly received. We know virtually nothing about the personal relationship of the two men. The fact that McLennan took Morgan to meet Maine indicates that they knew each other, and in a letter to Maine, written in the year before his death, McLennan stated that he was still working on a refutation of *Ancient Law*, that he would very much like to meet and talk about it with Maine, but that ill health prevented him.[127] However, there is no evidence which implies that McLennan had any personal animosity towards Maine.

Maine, for his part, paid little attention to the criticism of McLennan until after the latter's death. In *Village-Communi-*

125. Ibid., pp. ix–xi.
126. George Feaver, *From Status to Contract* (London, 1969) contains much information about Maine's political ideas. For further discussion of Maine's theories and their relation to his political ideology see H. Orenstein, "The Ethnological Theories of Henry Sumner Maine," *American Anthropologist* 70 (1968): 264–76.
127. Letter of 21 October 1880 (London School of Economics, Letters [10] *Maine Collection*). Andrew Lang, in letter 14 (undated) of the same collection, wrote to Maine saying that there was a lot of good in McLennan's work and that even if one did not agree with him it had to be admitted that he had put together a large amount of invaluable material. Lang goes on to say that it would be a shame to allow this material to be dissipated and that once he has finished his present work he would be willing to edit McLennan's notes. Lang was presumably unaware that Donald McLennan had taken on this task.

ties in the East and West (1871) he made some indirect and slighting remarks on both McLennan's and Lubbock's positions,[128] and in *The Early History of Institutions* (1874) there are only two brief references to *Primitive Marriage*. In *Early Law and Custom* (1883), after McLennan's death, he devoted a complete chapter to theories of primitive society, in which he claimed that he had been misunderstood in *Ancient Law* and that it had not been his intention to "determine the absolute origin of human society";[129] so that many of the criticisms of McLennan and Morgan were invalid. However, it was not until after the posthumous publication of *The Patriarchal Theory* that Maine was stung into making a far more violent (if anonymous) retort.[130] Even so, there is no particular reason to believe that there was any personal animosity between Maine and McLennan, and as Donald McLennan points out his brother's attempts to refute Maine's standpoint can be understood simply as an impersonal attack on the most prominent expounder and representative of the orthodox ideas which McLennan wished to dispel.

In summary, while much of this is speculative, the absence of any mention of *Ancient Law* and of any trace of the ideas which were to emerge two years later in *Primitive Marriage* in McLennan's review article (1863) on Indian ethnographies offers the strongest circumstantial evidence for the supposition that Maine was the major influence in the growth of McLennan's thought. The confirmatory but unanswerable question is: when exactly did McLennan read *Ancient Law*?

128. Maine, *Village-Communities in the East and West*, 3d ed. (London: John Murray, 1876). On p. 16 he writes of Lubbock and McLennan that they "have shown that the first steps of mankind towards civilization were taken from a condition in which assemblages of men followed practices which are not found to occur universally even in animal nature." Feaver also notes that Maine preferred to make the most important answers to his critics indirectly and discreetly—see *From Status to Contract*, p. 303, n. 17.

129. Maine, *Dissertations on Early Law and Custom* (London: John Murray, 1883), p. 192.

130. Maine, "The Patriarchal Theory," *The Quarterly Review* 163 (1886): 181–209. This is not a signed article, but it is attributed to Maine by M. E. Grant Duff, *Sir Henry Maine: a Brief Memoir of His Life* (London: John Murray, 1892), p. 67.

V

It cannot be said that *Primitive Marriage* made any immediate impact—it received neither popular acclaim nor censure. A contemporary reviewer in *The Athenaeum*—perhaps distracted by the misleading subtitle—missed the point of the work, and his review is marked by noncommittal bewilderment.[131] McLennan was better served by his reviewer in *The Saturday Review*—who, although criticizing him for his ignorance of physiology (stating that if matrilineal descent was predominant everybody would become progressively more feminine), at least concluded that "Mr. McLennan has opened a new path in historical research." [132] McLennan's professional colleagues were initially more responsive: Lubbock described it as an "excellent book";[133] and Tylor, while reserving his opinion about McLennan's correctness, was enthusiastic about his method, writing of it as the "introduction of the scientific method of induction from observed facts" as contrasted with the old "dogmatic *a priori* way which is so intensely unsatisfactory to the modern schools of natural sciences." [134] The attitude of McLennan's colleagues hardened, and many of the ideas contained in *Primitive Marriage* came in for a string of criticisms, to which, as we have already noticed, he responded with almost fanatical ferocity. It is worth considering briefly the fate of some of the ideas contained in *Primitive Marriage* since it is only by this means that we can evaluate McLennan's part in the development of anthropological thought.

The earliest criticisms of marriage by capture were not so

131. Anonymous review of J. F. McLennan's *Primitive Marriage,* in *The Athenaeum* (18 March 1865), pp. 376–77.

132. Anonymous review of J. F. McLennan's *Primitive Marriage,* in *The Saturday Review* 19 (25 February 1865): 232–34.

133. Sir John Lubbock, "The Early Condition of Man," *The Anthropological Review* 6 (1868): 1–21.

134. E. B. Tylor, "Phenomena of the Higher Civilization Traceable to a Rudimental Origin among Savage Tribes," *The Anthropological Review* 5 (1867): 303–18. While initially uncertain about McLennan's correctness, Tylor later came to accept his criticisms of the Patriarchal Theory (see Tylor's review of J. F. McLennan's *The Patriarchal Theory*, in *The Athenaeum* [30 May 1885], pp. 689–90).

much criticisms of the institution as such but, in the case of Spencer, of its cause[135] and, in the case of Lubbock who regarded marriage by capture as the origin of exogamy and not the latter as the cause of the former, of its place in the evolutionary scheme.[136] Starcke, however, pointed out that Lubbock had confused marriage by capture with the "symbol" of it and had thus misunderstood McLennan's argument,[137] but at the same time he questioned McLennan's reliance on such symbols and declared that one must be very careful "in identifying a given symbol with a definite previous practice." [138] In the case of marriage by capture he felt that McLennan had failed to do this, and suggested that there might well be other ways of interpreting such a ceremony; his own idea was that "the grief of seeing the old bonds relaxed or broken is expressed in the bride's lament, and it can find no more fitting symbol than in the resistance offered by her kinsfolk. . . ." [139] Wake had at the same period independently put forward an even better interpretation by suggesting that marriage by capture symbolized the transfer of jural authority.[140] Thus within a few years of McLennan's death there existed an explanation of the form of marriage by capture which no longer relied on a conjectural historical relationship between fact and form.

The place of female infanticide in McLennan's evolutionary scheme came in for an even earlier battery of devastating and not so devastating criticism. In the latter category must be included Lubbock's claim that male infanticide was as common as female infanticide since the lower races did not have

135. As Westermarck was to put it succinctly at a later date: "Whilst according to McLennan the custom of capture was due to a scarcity of women, it was according to Spencer due to the vanity of the men." (*The History of Human Marriage* [London, 1921], vol. 2, p. 167.)

136. Sir John Lubbock, *The Origin of Civilisation and the Primitive Condition of Man* (London, 1870), pp. 70–71.

137. C. N. Starcke, *The Primitive Family* (New York, 1894), p. 215. (This work was first published in German as *Die primitive Familie* [Leipzig, 1888], and the English translation was first published in London in 1889.)

138. Ibid., p. 213.

139. Ibid., p. 218.

140. Wake, *Marriage and Kinship*, p. 431.

the forethought and prudence to distinguish between the sexes,[141] while agreeing with McLennan that the prevalence of female infanticide was the result of economic and/or defensive necessity.[142] The earliest (1876) and one of the most damaging critics of McLennan's reliance on the institution of female infanticide as a necessary stage of social evolution was Herbert Spencer, who pointed out that in primitive societies the higher death rate of men would balance out female infanticide so that there would be no shortage of women,[143] and that if all tribes practiced female infanticide they would all be equally short of women.[144] Similar criticisms were voiced at the same time by Wilken.[145]

For McLennan, the shortage of women caused by female infanticide did not give rise merely to marriage by capture but also to polyandry, another of the essential stages of his evolutionary framework, and this was another of the features of *Primitive Marriage* which proved unacceptable to his critics. Lubbock gave no place to polyandry in his evolutionary scheme, and except where the evidence was conclusive regarded it as "laxness of morality" rather than as an institutionalized form of marriage.[146] Spencer was unwilling to accept polyandry as a universal stage in social evolution and regarded it simply as one option among all the possible forms of marriage.[147] Starcke, after reviewing the evidence, concluded that there were no grounds for assuming that polyandry was a development from a condition of sexual promiscuity or that it was a universal form of marriage.[148] Morgan criticized McLennan's view on the type and prevalence of polyandrous unions but only to defend his own (equally wrong) ideas about this in-

141. Lubbock, *Origin of Civilisation*, p. 70.
142. Ibid., p. 93.
143. Herbert Spencer, *The Principles of Sociology*, 3d ed. (New York, 1895), vol. 1, p. 616.
144. Ibid., p. 618.
145. See p. xxxiii, Editor's Introduction to the 1967 edition of Wake's *The Development of Marriage and Kinship*.
146. Lubbock, *Origin of Civilisation*, p. 101.
147. Spencer, *Principles*, p. 645.
148. Starcke, *Primitive Family*, pp. 139–40.

stitution.[149] However, it was Wake, although the fact barely received recognition until 1967, who provided the most thorough criticism of the whole of McLennan's argument and who set out to show that "the hypotheses of Dr. M'Lennan and Dr. Morgan, differing so widely from each other as they do, are both fundamentally erroneous." [150]

VI

At this point, the reader may well be wondering if a new edition of *Primitive Marriage* is really justified. The summary of McLennan's argument and the early fate of some of the basic elements in it make this a legitimate question. However, the facts that McLennan was almost entirely wrong and that to the modern reader his arguments may appear ridiculous is not sufficient reason to condemn his works. These can be defended on several grounds. First, McLennan can be excused, if not defended, because of the nature of the ethnographic material on which he depended. A glance at the works he cites will be enough to make this point. Many of them are the writings of classical or medieval authors and the rest the accounts and tales of travelers, soldiers, and sailors; today not one of them would be regarded as an adequate source of ethnographic evidence. Second, there are certain ideas contained both in *Primitive Marriage* and in his later writings which have proved to be of lasting importance. The most striking example of this is his recognition and naming of exogamy and endogamy, though it is fair to say that McLennan never really understood the workings of the marriage arrangements he had named. This in the first place arose from his failure to define the social groupings to which he was referring, which led to an obstinate refusal to see that exogamous and endogamous boundaries coexist within the same society. It is interesting that Spencer, who equally had no experience of primitive

149. L. H. Morgan, *Ancient Society* (New York, 1877), pp. 516–17.
150. Wake, *Marriage and Kinship*, p. 1. Wake, however, who had met McLennan in 1877 and had thereafter corresponded with him, also states that if McLennan had lived it might not have been necessary to write *The Development of Marriage and Kinship.*

societies, although criticizing McLennan's use of his terms, did not demonstrate any greater understanding of what the distinction between exogamy and endogamy might mean for people's social organization.[151] Indeed it was left to Morgan to indicate the true relationship of exogamy and endogamy.[152] After this, few commentators failed to agree with Morgan.

However, if Morgan was right about exogamy and endogamy, McLennan evened the score in their argument about the meaning of relationship terms, even if in denying Morgan's assumption that they were indicative of a biological relationship, he went too far in claiming that "they are barren of consequences except indeed as comprising a code of courtesies and ceremonial addresses in social intercourse."[153] McLennan has never received the unanimous support for his assumption about the nature of relationship categories that Morgan has for his clear description of the relationship of exogamy and endogamy, but it would be wrong not to regard them as seminal ideas on which we are still not agreed today. The nature of kinship categories and the source of incest prohibitions and the relationship of incest to exogamy are still matters of professional concern and dispute—as indeed are other topics, such as fabricated genealogies and the relationship between marriage rule and rule of descent, which McLennan introduced as subjects worthy of examination.

Furthermore there are other ideas which are still present in anthropological writings whose source is to be found in the pages of *Primitive Marriage*. Thus for example one can trace Lévi-Strauss's distinction between harmonic and dysharmonic

151. Spencer, *Principles*, p. 629. "Nothing of much importance is to be said respecting exogamy and endogamy in their bearings on social life."

152. Morgan, *Ancient Society*, pp. 511–15. I would agree with Marett that Morgan won "not because he was the cleverer man, but simply because he could always overtrump his opponent's facts." (*Tylor* [London: Chapman and Hall, 1936], p. 180). Marett also points out that in the ethnographies which McLennan used there is no consistent usage in the terms which the various authors applied to social groupings. Morgan, from his own field experience, could hardly have failed to appreciate the relationship between exogamy and endogamy.

153. McLennan (1876), p. 366.

regimes back through Durkheim[154] to McLennan's realization
that if kinship is traced through women and is symbolized by
totemic allegiance then marriage by capture will introduce
into the horde women whose offspring will be available for
marriage; it will result in what McLennan calls a heterogeneous
society.

In McLennan the heterogeneous society cannot be separated
from the ideas of matriliny, of clans, of exogamy, and of
totemism and the close relationship among these elements. Indeed the responsibility for the lasting arguments about totemism, and its assumed relationship with exogamous clans which
were in the first place matrilineal, can be squarely laid on
McLennan's shoulders, although the great influence that these
ideas had can to a great degree be attributed to the use made
of them by Robertson Smith. Robertson Smith, a close friend
and disciple of McLennan, believed that "the general principles
of the hypothesis, as laid down by McLennan, are not . . .
likely to be shaken."[155] He used McLennan's evolutionary
scheme in his study, *Kinship and Marriage in Early Arabia*
and this work, together with other writings, served to make
many of McLennan's ideas respectable. The influence was very
considerable, and even a thinker of Durkheim's caliber failed
to question the assumptions about the coherence of exogamy,
totemism, and matriclans.[156] Although the criticisms of evolu-

154. Cf. C. Lévi-Strauss, *The Elementary Structures of Kinship;* and
E. Durkheim, "La prohibition de l'inceste et ses origines," *L'Année
sociologique* 1 (1896–97): 1–70.

155. W. Robertson Smith, *Kinship and Marriage in Early Arabia*
(Cambridge University Press, 1885), pp. viii–ix. For more about Robert-
son Smith and his friendship with McLennan see Black and Chrystal,
William Robertson Smith.

156. Indeed Durkheim went to extraordinary lengths to protect this
assumption (see, for example, "Sur le totémisme," *L'Année sociologique*
5 (1900–1901): 82–121; and "Sur l'organisation matrimoniale des
sociétés australiennes," *L'Année sociologique* 8 (1903–4): 118–47), but
one must remember that on it rested his whole theory of religion. A few
years before, Tylor had written of McLennan's ideas on totemism that
there would be no need to criticize them but for the fact that they
carried such authority they induced "modern writers to repeat even his
conjectures as established principles." ("Remarks on Totemism, with
Especial Reference to Some Modern Theories Respecting It," *Journal of
the Anthropological Institute* n.s., 1 [1898]: 138–48.)

tionists and conjectural historians made by the functional school of anthropologists eradicated, among professional anthropologists, the idea of a social evolution that necessarily advanced from matriliny to patriliny, or from matriarchy to patriarchy, it still retains a hold not merely at a popular level but even among those who should know better.[157]

However, the influence of McLennan through Robertson Smith was not entirely baneful, since, as Robertson Smith acknowledged, it was McLennan who drew attention to the "intimate relation between religion and the fundamental structure of society which is so characteristic of the ancient world, and that the truth of the hypothesis can be tested by observations of the social organisation as well as the beliefs and practices of early races." [158] The relationship to which Robertson Smith refers is that between totemism (religion) and clan (social organization), and even if McLennan himself did not so clearly formulate the relationship as Robertson Smith did, the latter, as he so explicitly declares, found the idea in McLennan's work.

Thus there are in *Primitive Marriage* and elsewhere in McLennan's writings the seeds of many topics which are still of central concern to social anthropologists, and for this reason alone a new edition of McLennan is fully justified. But besides these individual and separate notions which have become the central themes of our discipline, there are other more general features of the work which qualify it to stand as a classic in anthropology.

First, there is a matter of method; as Evans-Pritchard has pointed out, *Primitive Marriage* is "the first really systematic attempt to make a comparative study of primitive societies." [159]

157. See Robert Graves, *The Greek Myths*, 2 vols. (London: Penguin edition, 1964), vol. 1, pp. 13–17, where it is assumed that the myths can only be interpreted as reflecting a change from matriarchy to patriarchy and that the Nairs are "the most primitive matrilineal society."

158. Robertson Smith, *Kinship and Marriage*, p. 223.

159. E. E. Evans-Pritchard, "The Comparative Method in Social Anthropology," L. T. Hobhouse Memorial Trust Lecture, no. 33 (London: The Athlone Press, 1963), p. 4. Maine, however, complained that McLennan neither understood nor used the comparative method (review

Furthermore his method was truly sociological, since he was trying to explain social institutions in terms of one another, to demonstrate their interdependence. That he was wrong is of very little importance when placed alongside what he was trying to do and the way in which he was trying to do it. An anonymous obituary writer was just in his remark that "Mr. M'Lennan may almost be said to have founded a new science," [160] and in some ways he deserves more than Tylor the title of "father of anthropology."

The other point about McLennan which should make him deserve our esteem is that he had a new and an original thought. Once again, the fact that his idea was wrong is not the important thing, and his idea of a matrilineal origin of social life is no worse as a theory than the patriarchal one which was the conventionally accepted idea about the origin of society until the second half of the nineteenth century. Indeed, it is only by the questioning of conventional wisdom with new sets of ideas that the boundaries of knowledge can be widened. McLennan was ideally suited for the part he was to play; a man with an original idea, with a willingness to propound it tenaciously, an immediate and violent reaction to the slightest criticism, and a crusading intent to destroy all opposition. His ideas received the attention he sought for them;[161] and al-

---

of J. F. McLennan's *The Patriarchal Theory,* in *The Quarterly Review* 162 [1886]: 199–201).

160. Obituary, *The Athenaeum* (25 June 1881), p. 851.

161. Some commentators' acclamation of McLennan was profuse. Elie Reclus, in a review article of Bachofen's *Das Mutterrecht* and McLennan's *Studies in Ancient History* (1876), declared that the two works complemented each other and together answered all their critics. He wrote of McLennan that "he adhered closely to logic and good sense, and to facts chiefly borrowed from contemporary history. His conclusions were presented in clear precise language; his argument was both sober and vigorous. Wherever he aimed he hit the mark." ("Female kinship and maternal filiation," *The Radical Review* [August 1877]). While H. Hale in a review of the second edition of *Studies in Ancient History* went so far as to describe it thus: "The grace of diction, the profound scholarship, and the stimulating originality of thought, displayed in the work, combine to make it one of the classics of modern science." (*Science* 8 [27 December 1886]: 569–70). He was describing the second edition of a work ten years old which contained unrevised material ten years older than that.

though he was not right, he showed his adversaries also to be wrong. He started people thinking, and we are still thinking about McLennan's thoughts today.

As a final justification for the reissue of this work, one can point out that it, together with Morgan's *Systems of Consanguinity and Affinity* and *Ancient Society* and Wake's *The Development of Marriage and Kinship*, forms an important stage in the history of ideas in general and in the development of anthropological thought in particular. Morgan's and Wake's works have recently been reprinted,[162] and the present appearance of *Primitive Marriage* completes a logical set.

VII

This introduction must close with a few notes about this reissue of *Primitive Marriage*. The text is the unabridged 1865 edition,[163] but certain alterations have been made, the most important of which has been the complete resetting of the text. In conjunction with this it has been refolioed, the footnotes have been numbered throughout each chapter in place of the original symbols, and obvious typographical and orthographical errors corrected. The main tasks in the editing of this volume have been the preparation of the index and the bibliography. The original index was judged to be inadequate for modern professional purposes and bibliographical information was restricted to the information contained in the footnotes. The preparation of the bibliography entailed considerable work because McLennan was far from careful about his references, many of which are scanty and too many wrong.[164] The names of authors were often slightly misspelled—for ex-

162. Morgan's *Ancient Society*, ed. L. A. White; (Harvard University Press, 1964) and *Systems of Consanguinity and Affinity* (Humanities Press, New York, 1966). Wake's *The Development of Marriage and Kinship*, ed. R. Needham (University of Chicago Press, 1967).

163. It appeared in February of that year and cost 12s. 6d. (*The English Catalogue of Books for 1865* [London, 1866], p. 35).

164. Some help in this task was obtained from a copy of a sale room catalogue which exists in the Bodleian Library, Oxford. It is *A Catalogue of Miscellaneous Books Including Portion of the Library of the Late J. F. McLennan, Esq. (Author of Primitive Marriage)*. The sale took place in London on 13 and 14 December 1906.

ample, Bergman for Bergmann, Hanthausen for Haxthausen, and Pritchard instead of Prichard—although one can offer as a partial excuse the difficulty of a printer in setting from handwriting. All such simple mistakes have been corrected without comment, but in cases of grosser error or omission the correction has been placed in square brackets. Where optional spellings exist, I have usually followed the names as entered in the *British Museum Reading Room Catalogue of Printed Books.* Furthermore, where, as on p. 83 of *Primitive Marriage,* a reference such as *Asi. Res.* Vol. iii, p. 35 (it should be p. 28) occurs, it appears in the bibliography as *Asiatick Researches,* vol. 3, and is cross-referenced to the particular author, who in this case is John Eliot.

In some cases McLennan has failed to give the edition to which he is referring, and in others has given the author and page number in the reference but not the title of the work. As far as possible I have tried to ascertain which edition McLennan used; but where this has not proved practicable, I have taken an edition published in the years just previous to the appearance of *Primitive Marriage.* Accordingly, it has not proved feasible to make a thorough check of McLennan's page references, although those which were looked up in the course of preparing the bibliography were found generally to be correct.

Some further interesting additions which it has been possible to make in this edition are the photographs of the busts of McLennan and of his signature. The frontispiece portrays the bust which his daughter presented to Aberdeen University in 1918 and which now stands in their Museum. I am grateful to the University of Aberdeen for permission to include this photograph and to Mr. A. T. Hall, deputy university librarian, for various information about McLennan, including the existence of the bust, and for arranging to have it photographed. Plate 1 depicts the bust of McLennan at Trinity College, Cambridge, which is by J. Hutchison and dated Edinburgh, 1892. I am grateful to Trinity College for permission to include a photograph of their bust in this new edition of *Primitive Marriage* and to Mr. A. Halcrow, the college's sub-librarian, who took the photograph. McLennan's signature is taken from a letter to Sir John Lubbock, dated 11 October 1867 and written from South Park, Reigate; it is reproduced by kind permission of the Trustees of the British Museum.

I received help from a number of people among whom I would like to single out for particular thanks J. H. Andrews of Dublin University for information from the Larcom papers, W. E. Fredeman of the University of British Columbia for the Rossetti reference to McLennan, and Mrs. Candy Shweder who typed the final draft. My thanks are further due to Dr. Rodney Needham who proved a constant and attentive source of encouragement; both he and Professor Evans-Pritchard read this introduction in draft form, and I readily acknowledge their comments. Finally, I am also grateful to the University of Chicago Press for allowing me to edit this work which has proved both an enjoyable and rewarding task.

A Bibliography of
John Ferguson McLennan

1857. "Law," *Encyclopaedia Britannica*, 8th ed., 13: 253–79.

1860a. "Some Recollections of an Old Street." *Macmillan's Magazine* 1 (April): 431–39. (Signed: Richard Futiloe).*

1860b. *Scottish Art and Artists in 1860*. Edinburgh. (Signed: Iconoclast).

1861. "Marriage and Divorce—the Law of England and Scotland." *North British Review* 35 (August): 187–218. (Anonymous).*

1863. "Hill Tribes in India." *North British Review* 38 (May): 392–422. (Anonymous).*

1864. "Scottish Criminal Statistics." In *Transactions of the National Association for the Promotion of Social Science, Edinburgh Meeting, 1863*. Edited by G. W. Hastings, pp. 384–94. London.

1865. *Primitive Marriage: An Inquiry into the Origin of the Form of Capture in Marriage Ceremonies*. Edinburgh: Adam and Charles Black.

1866a. "Concerning Easy-writing." *Argosy* 1 (April): 325–35.

1866b. "Kinship in Ancient Greece." *The Fortnightly Review* 4 (April): 569–88.

1866c. "Kinship in Ancient Greece." *The Fortnightly Review* 4 (May): 682–91.

1866d. "Bride-Catching." *Argosy* 2 (July): 31–42.

1867a. *Memoir of Thomas Drummond, R.E., F.R.A.S., Under-*

* The authority for assigning these articles to McLennan is *The Wellesley Index to Victorian Periodicals, 1824–1900*, vol. 1.

Secretary to the Lord Lieutenant of Ireland, 1835–1840.
Edinburgh: Edmonston and Douglas.

1867b. "Scottish Criminal Statistics." Letter in *The Scotsman* (3 December), p. 2.

1868. "Totem." *Chamber's Encyclopaedia*, 1st ed., Supplement: 753–54.

1869a. "Tree and Serpent Worship." *Cornhill Magazine,* 19 (May): 626–40. (Anonymous.)*

1869b. "The Early History of Man." *North British Review* o.s., 50 (July): 516–49. (Anonymous.)*

1869c. "The Worship of Animals and Plants, Part I." *The Fortnightly Review* 6 (October): 407–27.

1869d. "The Worship of Animals and Plants, Part II." *The Fortnightly Review* 6 (November): 562–82.

1870. "The Worship of Animals and Plants, Part III." *The Fortnightly Review* 7 (February): 194–216.

1876. *Studies in Ancient History Comprising a Reprint of Primitive Marriage.* London: Bernard Quaritch. This volume also includes: "Kinship in Ancient Greece," pp. 235–309; "The Classificatory System of Relationships," pp. 329–407; "Bachofen's *Das Mutterrecht*," pp. 409–21; "Communal Marriage," pp. 423–49; and "Divisions of the Ancient Irish Family," pp. 451–507.

1877a. "The Levirate and Polyandry." *The Fortnightly Review* 21 (May): 694–707.

1877b. "Exogamy and Endogamy." *The Fortnightly Review* 21 (June): 884–95.

1885. *The Patriarchal Theory.* Edited and completed by Donald McLennan. London: Macmillan & Co.

1886. *Studies in Ancient History Comprising a Reprint of Primitive Marriage.* London: Macmillan & Co. (A new edition with notes by D. McLennan.)

1888. "The Origin of Exogamy." *English Historical Review* 3: 94–104. (With notes added by D. McLennan).

l

1896.   *Studies in Ancient History: The Second Series.* Edited
        by his widow and Arthur Platt. London: Macmillan &
        Co.

PRIMITIVE MARRIAGE

Preface

IN the course of some inquiries which I had been making into the early history of civil society, the meaning and origin of the Form of Capture in Marriage Ceremonies fell to be investigated. The subject being in itself curious, as well as obscure, and one which has never hitherto, so far as I am aware, been handled, I venture to lay the result of my investigation before the public, hoping that it may to some extent interest by its novelty. To the philosophic reader, I humbly submit my little book as an exercise in scientific history. If I am right in my conclusions as to the origin of the symbol of capture, my essay must be accepted as throwing new light on the primitive state. For it will be seen that the symbol is not peculiar to any of the families of mankind. It is at once Indo-European, Tauranian, and Semitic; and the frequency of its occurrence is such as strongly to suggest—what I incline to believe—that the phase of society in which it originated existed, at some time or other, almost everywhere. Indeed, so far as my inquiries into early social phenomena have extended, I have found such similarity, so many correspondences, so much sameness in the forms of life prevailing among the races usually considered distinct, that I have come to regard the ethnological differences of the several families of mankind as of little or no weight compared with what they have in common. The most that can be attributed to those differences is, that they have affected the rate of development of the families, and the character of the development itself, in some of its secondary aspects.

Apart from the interest attaching to the Form of Capture as pointing out what most probably was the primitive form of human association, it will be found to have an important bearing on several social problems which have hitherto remained unsolved. I think that the most important portions of my work are Chapters 8 and 9, in which the solution of some of these problems is attempted. These chapters, it will be seen, are strictly pertinent to the main subject of inquiry. In order to explain the appearance of the Form of Capture among endogamous peoples, it was necessary that I should examine the systems of kinship which anciently prevailed, and their influence on the structure of the primitive groups, so as to obtain a true view of the rise of caste and of endogamy.

I ought to mention that, in some cases, I have had much difficulty in ascertaining the proper names of places. For instance, Munniepore is sometimes written Munipur, and sometimes Mannipoor. In every such case I have followed the authority which I have had most frequent occasion to cite in regard to the place. I have farther to notice, that I have discarded the use of the signs ^ ‾ _ . ˈˆ˙˙, and so on, commonly employed to indicate the orthoepy of foreign words. Such signs are of no use to the unlearned; and, in the run of cases, the learned may be presumed not to require their assistance. Besides, I have not found much agreement, among writers, in the use of such signs. The word Ramayana, for example, is written Rámáyana by Professor Monier-Williams, Rāmāyaṇa by Dr. Muir, and Râmâyana by Professor Max Müller. In writing it simply Ramayana, I follow Mr. Tagore, in his recent translation of the "Vivada Chintamani," in which work, as in the present, the signs referred to are wholly discarded.

EDINBURGH, Jan. 6, 1865

1
Introductory: Legal Symbolism and Primitive Life

THE chief sources of information regarding the early history of civil society are, first, the study of races in their primitive condition; and, second, the study of the symbols employed by advanced nations in the constitution or exercise of civil rights. From these studies pursued together, we obtain, to a large extent, the power of classifying social phenomena as more or less archaic, and thus of connecting and arranging in their order the stages of human advancement.

None of the usual methods of historical inquiry conduct us back to forms of life so nearly primitive as many that have come down into our own times. The geological record, of course, exhibits races as rude as any now living, some perhaps even more so, but then it goes no farther than to inform us what food they ate, what weapons they used, and what was the character of their ornaments. More than this was not to be expected from that record, for it was not in its nature to preserve any memorials of those aspects of human life in which the philosopher is chiefly interested—of the family or tribal groupings, the domestic and political organisation. Again, the facts disclosed by philology as to the civil condition of the Indo-European race before its dispersion from its original headquarters,—the earliest, chronologically considered, which we possess respecting the *social* state of mankind,—cannot be said to tell us anything of the origin or early progress of civilization. Assuming the correctness of the generalization by which philologers have attempted to reconstruct the social economy of the Aryans, we find that people, at an unknown date before the dawn of tradition, occupying nearly the same point of advancement as that now occupied by the pastoral hordes of Kirghiz Tartary, and leading much the same sort of life. They had marriage laws regulating the rights and obligations of husbands and wives, of parents and children; they recognised the ties of blood through both parents; they had great flocks and herds, in defence of which they often did battle, and they lived under a patriarchal government with monarchical features. It is interesting—a short time ago we should have said surprising—to find that such progress had been so early made. But in all other respects this so-called revelation of philology is void of instruction. Those Aryan institutions are—to use the language of geology—postpliocene, separated by a long interval from the foundations of civil society, and throwing back upon them no light. Marriage laws, agnatic relationship, and kingly government, belong, in the order of development, to recent times.

For the features of primitive life, we must look, not to tribes of the Kirghiz type, but to those of Central Africa, the wilds of America, the hills of India, and the islands of the Pacific; with some of whom we find marriage laws unknown, the family system undeveloped, and even the only acknowledged blood-relationship that through mothers. These facts of to-day are, in a sense, the most ancient history. In the sciences of law and society, old means not old in chronology, but in structure: that is most archaic which lies nearest to the beginning of human progress considered as a development, and that is most modern which is farthest removed from that beginning.

And since the historical nations were so far advanced at the earliest dates to which even philology can lead us back, the scientific investigation of the progress of mankind must not deal with them, in the first instance, but with the very rude forms of life still existing, and the rudest of which we have accounts. The preface of general history must be compiled from the materials presented by barbarism. Happily, if we may say so, these materials are abundant. So unequally has the species been developed, that almost every conceivable phase of progress may be studied, as somewhere observed and recorded. And thus the philosopher, fenced from mistake, as to the order of development, by the interconnection of the stages and their shading into one another by gentle gradations, may draw a clear and decided outline of the course of human progress in times long antecedent to those to which even philology can make reference.

All honour to philology; but in the task of reconstructing the past, to which its professors declare themselves to be devoted, they must be contented to act as assistants rather than as principals.

We have said that the preface of general history must be compiled from materials presented by barbarism. Some may account it illogical to prefix a scheme of early progress formed on view of societies that have not yet advanced far, if at all, from savagery, to a scheme of further progress deduced from the written histories of nations whose origin and early training we are unacquainted with. But, in point of fact, it is not so. It is the best proof of the propriety of such a course—as well as of the continuity and uniform character of human progress —that we can trace everywhere, disguised under a variety of symbolical forms in the higher layers of civilization, the rude modes of life and forms of law with which the examination of the lower makes us familiar. Indeed, were these remarks not merely general and introductory to the investigation of the origin of one particular symbol, many instances of this correspondence between the higher and lower levels might be cited, to show that the symbolism of law in the light of a knowledge of primitive life, is the best key to unwritten history.

Of the value of that symbolism—of that reverence for the past to which it owes its origin—there will be occasion to say something hereafter. Meantime, we observe that, wherever we discover symbolical forms, we are justified in inferring that in the past life of the people employing them, there were corresponding realities; and if, among the primitive races which we examine, we find such realities as might naturally pass into such forms on an advance taking place in civility, then we may safely conclude (keeping within the conditions of a sound inference) that what these now are, those employing the symbols once were. History is thus made to ratify conclusions derived from the observation of rude tribes; while such observation, again, is made to furnish the key to many of the enigmas of history.

For it is not as regards unwritten history merely that the two sources of information specified at the outset are of importance. Apart from the tests of truth afforded by the minute knowledge of primitive modes of life and their classification as more or less archaic, nothing could be more delusive than written history itself. In Roman law, to take a convenient example, Confarreatio has the foremost place among the modes of constituting marriage. Usus is just mentioned in the twelve tables, which contain a provision against the wife coming into the Manus of her husband through Usus. Coemptio does not appear in the old law of Rome at all, nor is there any mention of it earlier than that by Gaius. But it can easily be shown that Usus and Coemptio come first in order of age, and Confarreatio later; that is to say, the two former are more archaic than the latter. Yet have recent learned writers, overlooking this fact and the meaning of legal symbolism, represented Usus and Coemptio as forms invented and introduced by the legislators of Rome, whereby the plebeians might have their wives in Manu, and enjoy the other advantages of Justae Nuptiae; Usus as an invention; and the fictitious sale in Coemptio as merely a device of legislative ingenuity. The true explanation of the late appearance of both Usus and the fictitious sale in the Roman law, is this—that the law at first was not that of the whole people but of a limited aristocracy, who, with a Sabine king and priesthood, adopted the Sabine religious ceremony of marriage; that the law long totally ignored the life and usages of the mass, and that *their* modes of marrying and giving in marriage began to appear, and to make their mark in the law, only on the popular element in the city becoming of importance. Instead of marriage *per coemptionem* being the invention of legislators, it was of spontaneous popular growth, and must have been as old as the establishment of peaceful relations between tribes and families. All fictions, or nearly all, have had their germs in facts; became fictions or merely symbolical forms afterwards. And that the fictitious sale was originally an actual sale and purchase, cannot be doubted by any one who knows that marriage by the form of actual sale has prevailed almost universally among rude populations.

We see in the case of the Roman law how incomplete must necessarily be the history of the law of a country, as written on the face of it. The law is at first that of the dominant and presumably the most advanced classes—the literates, warriors, and statesmen; the rest of the community are beyond its pale, a law unto themselves. When the levelling processes, by which the lower classes succeed in the long run in acquiring rights more or less equal, have gone on for some time, then the ruder customs followed by them before and since the commencement of the State appear in a modified form in what is now for the first time really becoming the law of the people. Civility seems suddenly to assume the garb and the air, and to use the gutturals of barbarism; legal processes are gone through with the frantic howls and gesticulations of armed Ojibeways; and while all this, to those who are ignorant of primitive times, seems mere idle pantomime, sometimes silly, sometimes odd, sometimes puzzling by its intricacy, to those who are prepared to receive their suggestions, the forms employed are pregnant with meaning and instruction. Fortunately all the nations in the world have not advanced in civility *pari passu;* and what is pantomime with one people, we discern to be grimmest reality with another. Were it not for this inequality of development, in what mysteries would the history of the race be enveloped! What Michelet calls the poetry of law would have to be received as such simply; as so many grotesqueries or graces introduced into the ways of life to satisfy the popular fancy. As it is, however, the so-called poetry of law, the symbolic forms that appear in a code or in popular customs, tell us as certainly of the early usages of a people, as the rings in the transverse section of a tree tell of its age.

The Libripens, with his scales, officiating at a will or act of adoption, seems out of place; but his presence illustrates the source whence all ideas of formal dispositions were derived—the sale of fungibles. So does an old form of process preserved by Gaius—the Legis Actio Sacramenti of the Romans—prove that cultivated people to have been at one time *in pari casu* as regards the administration of justice with many races which we find ignorant of legal proceedings, and dependent for the settlement of their disputes on force of arms or the good offices of neutral parties interfering as arbiters.

So far, briefly, of the importance of the symbolism of law and of the study of races in their primitive condition. What follows is an attempt at a practical exemplification in a new direction of the aid derivable from these sources in the task of unveiling the past.

2

The Form of Capture in Marriage Ceremonies

IN the whole range of legal symbolism there is no symbol more remarkable than that of capture in marriage ceremonies—the origin of which it is our purpose to investigate—nor is there any the meaning of which has been less studied. So far as we know, neither has the extent to which it prevails been made the subject of inquiry; nor its significance the subject of thought. In two cases, indeed, the occurrence of the symbol could not fail to receive some attention. But, naturally, it did not lie in the way of the historians of either Greece or Rome to examine the matter very minutely, or to follow up the suggestions which, upon examination, it might have yielded, as to the early condition of the Dorians or Latins. Accordingly, the custom has been accepted as meaning no more than Festus said it did among the Romans, than Müller says it did among the Spartans; as indicating nothing at Rome but the popular appreciation of the good fortune of Romulus in the rape of the Sabines;[1] as indicating, at Sparta, the feeling that a young woman "could not surrender her freedom and virgin purity unless compelled by the violence of the stronger sex."[2] It is surprising that writers so acute should have rested content with such explanations, and that their views should have been so generally adopted. The theory of Festus we shall have occasion to notice hereafter: of that of Müller we observe that before we can entertain it, we must suppose that in the exceedingly lax community of the Spartans, or at least within certain of the tribes composing that community, there had been an early period of austere virtue, the tradition of which was still so influential as to compel the Spartans to observe in their marriages this custom as the shadow of their former delicacy. Now, of the existence of such a period of prudery among the ancient

1. Festus, De Verborum Significatione—Rapi.
2. Müller's "Dorians," Book iv., c. iv., sec. 2; and see "Rawlinson's Notes," Herod., Book vi. 65.

Dorians, or among the Pelasgi, or the Achaeans, there is not a tittle of evidence. On the contrary, such evidence as we have points to the Lacedaemonian customs as having been an improvement on ancient practice. Savages are not remarkable for delicacy of feeling in matters of sex, and the wandering hordes, who in succession overran the Peloponnesus, were no better than savages when they first come under our observation.[3] Again, no case can be cited of a primitive people among whom the seizure of brides is rendered necessary by maidenly coyness. On the contrary, it might be shown, were it worth while to deal seriously with this view, that women among rude tribes are usually depraved, and inured to scenes of depravity from their earliest infancy. In this state of the facts, it is remarkable that any one should have been satisfied with so improbable an explanation.

Rejecting, then, the primitive prudery hypothesis, which requires for its basis a declension from ancient standards of purity—of the existence of which we have no evidence—we proceed to examine the various phases in which the symbol of capture is presented. We shall find it in places far from classic ground, and pointing, in all its varieties, so steadily to the true theory of its origin, that the mere exhibition of its phases will lead the reader to anticipate much of what we have to say on the subject. In order to see what is the precise state of the facts with which we have to deal, it is necessary to say something of the nature of the symbol, and to adduce at some length such accounts of it as we find in our authorities.

The symbol of capture occurs whenever, after a contract of marriage, it is necessary for the constitution of the relation of husband and wife that the bridegroom or his friends should go through the form of feigning to steal the bride, or carry her off from her friends by superior force. The marriage is agreed upon by bargain, and the theft or abduction follows as a concerted matter of form, to make valid the marriage. The test, then, of the presence of the symbol in any case is, that the capture is concerted, and is preceded by a contract of marriage.

3. They were certainly as savage as the Khonds, with whom they agreed in cultivating a religion requiring human sacrifices.

If there is no preceding contract, the case is one of actual abduction.

So far of the nature of the symbol. We proceed to examine the instances of its occurrence. That the form was observed in the marriages of the Dorians, and was, equally with betrothal, requisite as a preliminary of marriage, rests chiefly on the authority of Herodotus and Plutarch.[4] The evidence of Herodotus is indirect, and is contained in the well-known passage in which he explains how Demaratus robbed Lestychides of his bride Percalus, to whom he had been betrothed—*forestalling* him in carrying her off and marrying her.[5] The case was one of actual abduction; but the language of Herodotus implies that it remained for Lestychides, in order to make Percalus his wife, that he should go through the form of carrying her off. With this must be conjoined the express statement of Plutarch,[6] that the Spartan bridegroom always carried off the bride by feigned violence. He says, indeed, *by violence;* but at the same time he shews that the seizure was made by friendly concert between the parties. These passages must be held sufficiently to prove that the custom existed at Sparta. It is equally certain that it was observed at Rome,[7] in the plebeian marriages which were not constituted by Confarreatio or Coemptio. The bridegroom and his friends—the time agreed upon having arrived —invaded the house of the bride, and carried off the lady with feigned force from the lap of her mother, or of her nearest female relation if the mother were dead or absent. The seizure is vividly described by Apuleius[8] in the story of the Captive Damsel, in which he is understood to have had the plebeian form of marriage in view. The lady, narrating how she had been carried off, says that her mother having dressed her becomingly in nuptial apparel, was loading her with kisses, and looking forward to a future line of descendants, when on a sudden a band of robbers, armed like gladiators, rushed in

4. Müller's "Dorians," *ut supra.*
5. "Herodotus," B. vi., 65.
6. "Life of Lycurgus."
7. Festus, *ut supra*—Rapi: Pothier, Pandectae, etc., App., Title II. book xxiii.
8. Apuleius, de Asino Aureo, Book iv.

with glittering swords, made straight for her chamber in a compact column, and, without any struggle or resistance whatever on the part of the servants, tore her away half dead with fear from the bosom of her trembling mother. The custom is said still to prevail to a great extent among the Hindus.[9] It may well do so, for we find what must, as we shall show, be held to be the form of capture, prescribed as a marriage ceremony to the Hindus in the Sutras.[10] It prevails among the Khonds in the hill tracts of Orissa. The marriage being agreed upon, a feast, to which the families of the parties equally contribute, is prepared at the dwelling of the bride. "To the feast," says Major MacPherson,[11] "succeed dancing and song. When the night is far spent, the principals in the scene are raised by an uncle of each upon his shoulders, and borne through the dance. The burdens are suddenly exchanged, and the uncle of the youth disappears with the bride. The assembly divides into two parties; the friends of the bride endeavour to arrest, those of the bridegroom to cover her flight, and men, women, and children, mingle in mock conflict, which is often carried to great lengths." "On one occasion," says Major-General Campbell,[12]

> I heard loud cries proceeding from a village close at hand. Fearing some quarrel, I rode to the spot, and there I saw a man bearing away upon his back something enveloped in an ample covering of scarlet cloth; he was surrounded by twenty or thirty young fellows, and by them protected from the desperate attacks made upon him by a party of young women. On seeking an explanation of this novel scene, I was told that the man had just been married, and his precious burden was his blooming bride, whom he was conveying to his own village. Her youthful friends—as, it appears, is the custom—were seeking to regain possession of her, and hurled stones and bamboos at the head of the devoted

9. MacPherson's "Report upon the Khonds of the districts of Ganjam and Cuttack," p. 55. Calcutta, 1842.
10. "Indische Studien," p. 325. Edited by Dr. Weber. Berlin, 1862.
11. MacPherson's "Report," *ut supra*.
12. "Personal Narrative of Service, etc., in Khondistan," 1864, p. 44.

bridegroom, until he reached the confines of his own village.[13] Then the tables were turned, and the bride was fairly won; and off her young friends scampered, screaming and laughing, but not relaxing their speed till they reached their own village.

The custom may be presumed to prevail among the Koles, the Ghonds, and the other congeners of the Khonds; but we are without authority on the subject.

According to De Hell,[14] the form of capture is observed in the marriages of the noble or princely class among the Kalmucks. The price to be paid for the bride to her father having been fixed, the bridegroom sets out on horseback, accompanied by the chief nobles of the horde to which he belongs, to carry her off. "A sham resistance is always made by the people of her camp, in spite of which she fails not to be borne away on a richly caparisoned horse, with loud shouts and *feux de joie.*" Dr. Clarke describes the ceremony differently, and it is possible that it assumes different forms in the different nations of the Kalmucks. "The ceremony of marriage among the Kalmucks," he says,[15]

> is performed on horseback. A girl is first mounted, who rides off in full speed. Her lover pursues; if he overtakes her, she becomes his wife, and the marriage is consummated on the spot; after this she returns with him to his tent. But it sometimes happens that the woman does not wish to marry the person by whom she is pursued; in this case, she will not suffer him to overtake her. We were assured that no instance occurs of a Kalmuck girl being thus caught, unless she have a partiality to the pursuer. If she dislikes him, she rides, to use the language of English sportsmen, "neck or nought," until she has

13. The hurling of old shoes, etc., after the bridegroom among ourselves, *may be* a relic of a similar custom. It is a sham assault on the person carrying off the lady; and in default of any more plausible explanation, and we know of none such, it may fairly be considered as probable that it is the form of capture in its last stage of disintegration.

14. Xavier Hommaire de Hell, "Travels in the Steppes of the Caspian Sea." Lond. 1847, p. 259.

15. "Travels," etc., vol. i., p. 433.

completely effected her escape, or until her pursuer's horse becomes exhausted, leaving her at liberty to return, and to be afterwards chased by some more favoured admirer.

This ride for a wife is never undertaken till after the price for her has been fixed between the friends of the parties, the lover having to pay for as well as to catch her. The custom is not mentioned in the account of the Kalmucks by Pallas, who knew of their marriage customs only by hearsay. But it favours the supposition that there are varieties of the form in use among this people, that Bergmann[16] describes the ceremony somewhat differently from both Clarke and De Hell. The necessity for the appearance of using force is satisfied, according to Bergmann, by the act of putting the bride by force upon horseback when she is about to be conducted to the hut prepared for her by the bridegroom. And, indeed, we find the form reduced to this minimum of pretence in not a few cases. Thus in North Friesland,[17] a young fellow, called the bride-lifter, lifts the bride and her two bridesmaids upon the waggon in which the married couple are to travel to their home.

Among the Tunguzes and Kamchadales, a matrimonial engagement is not considered to be definitely concluded until the suitor has overcome his beloved by force, and torn her clothes—the maiden being bound by custom to defend her liberty to the utmost.[18] Also among the Bedouin Arabs it is necessary for the bridegroom to force the bride to enter his tent.[19] A similar custom existed among the French, at least in some provinces, in the 17th century.[20] In all the cases just mentioned the form assumed by the custom was analogous to the rule prescribed in the Sutras, where it was provided that at a certain vital stage of the marriage ceremony, *a strong man*

16. Bergmann's "Streifereien." Riga 1804, vol. 3, p. 145, *et seq.*
17. Weinhold, pp. 250, 251; and see the other authorities for like cases noted by Dr. Weber, "Indische Studien," *ut supra.*
18. "Travels in Siberia," Erman, vol. ii., p. 442—1848 (Cowley's trans.)
19. Burckhardt's "Notes on the Bedouins and Wahabys." Lond. 1830, vol. i., p. 108.
20. "Marriage Ceremonies," etc., Gaya, 2d ed. Lond. 1698, p. 30.

and the bridegroom should forcibly draw the bride and make her sit down on a red ox-skin.[21]

There is good ground for believing that the form of capture is observed in the marriage ceremonies of the Nogay Tartars. The rule which prohibits a Kalmuck bride from entering the yurt of her parents for a year or more after her marriage, and which is undoubtedly connected with the form of capture, prevails among the Nogais, as it does also among the Kirghiz. At any rate, we find the custom in the Caucasus in the immediate neighbourhood of the Nogais. The form which it assumes among the Circassians, indeed, closely resembles that observed in ancient Rome. The wedding is celebrated with noisy feasting and revelry, "in the midst of which the bridegroom has to rush in, and with the help of a few daring young men, to carry off the lady by force; and by this process she becomes his lawful wife." [22] The custom also prevailed till a recent date in Wales. Lord Kames[23] says that the following marriage ceremony was in his day, or at least had till shortly before been customary among the Welsh.

> On the morning of the wedding day, the bridegroom, accompanied with his friends on horseback, demands the bride. Her friends, who are likewise on horseback, give a positive refusal, upon which a mock scuffle ensues. The bride, mounted behind her nearest kinsman, is carried off and is pursued by the bridegroom and his friends, with loud shouts. It is not uncommon on such an occasion to see two or three hundred sturdy Cambro-Britons riding at full speed, crossing and jostling to the no small amusement of the spectators. When they have fatigued themselves and their horses, the bridegroom is suffered to overtake his bride. He leads her away in triumph, and the scene is concluded with feasting and festivity.

Some such picture we should have had from De Hell had he

21. "Indische Studien," *ut supra.*
22. Louis [Ludwig] Moser, "The Caucasus and its People." Lond. 1856, p. 31; and see Spencer's "Travels in Circassia." Lond. 1837, vol. ii. p. 375; and "Bell's Journal," vol. ii. p. 221. Lond. 1840.
23. "Sketches of the History of Man," Book 1., sec. 6, p. 449. Edin. 1807.

expanded his account of the mock scuffle among the Kalmucks of the hordes of the bride and bridegroom.

We have now found the custom in various parts of Europe and Asia; it occurs also in Africa and in America. Lord Kames vouches for the custom among the Inland Negroes.[24]

> When the preliminaries of the marriage are adjusted, the bridegroom with a number of his companions set out at night and surround the house of the bride as if intending to carry her off by force; she and her female attendants pretending to make all possible resistance, cry aloud for help, but no person appears.

Speke[25] mentions an incident which he observed in Karague, and which *may* have been the sequel to a capture. "At night," he says,

> I was struck by surprise to see a long noisy procession pass by where I sat, led by some men who carried on their shoulders a woman covered up in a blackened skin. On inquiry, however, I heard she was being taken to the hut of her espoused, where bundling fashion she would be put to bed; but it is only with virgins they take so much trouble.

Traces of the custom are indeed frequently met with in Africa, but in so distinct and marked a form as that mentioned by Lord Kames, we have not found it. His lordship has not given his authority. He mentions the custom, however, merely for its singularity, and apparently in ignorance of its connecting itself with any wide-spread practice of mankind, which demanded investigation. Among the primitive races throughout the whole continent of America traces of the form of capture (that is, customs seemingly of no significance, except in the light of this form) are of frequent occurrence. Among the people of Tierra del Fuego, however, the form itself appears almost in perfection. "As soon," says Captain Fitzroy, speaking of the Fuegians,[26]

24. "Sketches," etc., *ut supra.*
25. "Journal of the Discovery of the Source of the Nile," 1863, p. 198.
26. "Voyages of the Adventure and Beagle." Vol. ii., p. 182; 1839.

as a youth is able to maintain a wife by his exertions in fishing or bird-catching, *he obtains the consent of her relations,* and does some piece of work, such as helping to make a canoe, or prepare seal-skins, etc., for her parents. Having built or stolen a canoe for himself, he watches for an opportunity, and carries off his bride. If she is unwilling she hides herself in the woods, until her admirer is heartily tired of looking for her, and gives up the pursuit, but this seldom happens.

These are among the best marked instances of the Form with which we are acquainted.[27] The instances fix our attention especially upon a few geographical points. But nothing in nature stands by itself. Each example of the Form leads us to contemplate a great area over which the custom once prevailed, just as a fossil fish in rock on a hill-side forces us to conceive of the whole surrounding country as at one time under water. Were we to enumerate and examine all the customs which seem to us connected with the Form, we should be led into discussions foreign to our purpose, and there would be few primitive races with which we should not have to deal. Suffice it, that the Form which of old appeared so well defined in the peninsulas of Italy and Greece, may be traced thence, on the one hand, northwards through France and Britain, south-westwards through Spain, and north-eastwards through Prussia; on the other hand, northwards through ancient Thessaly and Macedonia, into the mountainous regions on the Black Sea and the Caspian; again, that the form which is perfect among the Kalmucks shades away into faint and fainter traces throughout almost all the races of the Mongolidae; that we may assume it of frequent occurrence in Africa, as it unquestionably was among the red men of America; that it occurs among the Hindus, and may be assumed to have been common among the aboriginal inhabitants of the plains of India, of whom we have a well-preserved specimen in the Khonds of Orissa.

27. The reader will find in the Appendix A, a marked example of the Form, occurring in Ireland, and several other examples occurring elsewhere, which the author has not thought it necessary to incorporate in the text.

3

The Origin of the Form of Capture

THE question now arises, what is the meaning and what the origin of a ceremony so widely spread, that already on the threshold of our inquiry, the reader must be prepared to find it connected with some universal tendency of mankind?

Those who approach the subject with minds undisturbed by the views of Festus and Müller will most naturally think, in the first instance, of an early period of lawlessness, in which it was with women as with other kinds of property, that he should take who had the power, and he should keep who could. And it is a trite fact, that women captured in war have universally, in barbarous times and countries, been appropriated as wives, or as worse. But little consideration is needed to see that the symbol implies much more than this; for it is impossible to believe that the mere lawlessness of savages should be consecrated into a legal symbol, or to assign a reason—could this be believed—why a similar symbol should not appear in transferences of other kinds of property. To a certain extent, indeed, the first impression must be held to be a correct one. We cannot escape the conclusion that there was a stage in the history of tribes observing this custom when wives were usually obtained by theft or force. And unless the practice of getting wives by theft or force was so general where it prevailed that we may say it was almost invariable, it is incredible that such an association should be established in the popular mind between marriage and the act of rapine, as would afterwards require the pretence of rapine to give validity to the ceremony of marriage. It must have been *the system* of certain tribes to capture women—necessarily the women of other tribes—for wives. But we may be sure that such a system could not have sprung out of the mere instinctive desire of savages to possess objects cherished by a foreign tribe; it must have had a deeper source—to be sought for in their circumstances, their ideas of kinship, their tribal arrangements.

The fact that among savage tribes—whose normal relations with each other are those of war—a man could get a woman of a foreign tribe for his wife only by carrying her off, cannot, *by itself*, explain a symbolism which is so well established, so invariable, where it occurs at all. Where savages had women of their own whom they might marry, captive women would naturally become slaves or concubines rather than wives; the men would find their wives, or their chief wives, within the tribe; and the capture of women could never become so important in connection with marriage as to furnish a symbolism for all marriages to a later time. It may be doubted whether, in the circumstances supposed, the form of capture would, in a great number of cases, be bequeathed to more peaceful and friendly generations, even in the case of intertribal marriages —in which only the form could be expected to appear; and at any rate these, when first made subjects of friendly compact, would be too infrequent for their ceremonies to override those which were indigenous, and to be transferred into the general marriage law. Much more likely is it that indigenous marriage forms should be employed in the celebration of intertribal marriages when they occurred. It is *a fortiori*, that in the circumstances which we have been considering—those of tribes among which as among civilized peoples, the law of marriage is *matrimonium liberum*—no *system* of capturing women for wives could have arisen.

What circumstances then, what social idea, existing among rude tribes, could produce a system of capturing the women of foreign tribes for wives? It will be convenient, that before we make the answer we have to offer to this question, we should consider the condition, in respect of marriage, of a class of tribes with which we believe this system did *not* originate.

It is clear, that if members of a family or tribe *are forbidden* to intermarry with members of other families or tribes, and free to marry among themselves, there is not room for fraud or force in the constitution of marriage. The bridegroom and bride will live together in amity among their common relatives. With the consent of her relations, a woman will become the wife of a suitor peaceably. If a suitor forces her, or carries her off against her will or that of her friends, he must separate from these to escape their vengeance. It follows that, among tribes of this class, which we shall call *endogamous tribes*,[1] betrothal followed by cohabitation at first, and, at a more advanced stage, betrothal and a religious or other formal ceremony of appropriation of the spouses to one another, are the natural modes of marriage. To the practice of such tribes are to be referred the two modes of constituting marriage of which the Roman usus and confarreatio may be taken as the types. These are at any rate the forms appropriate to marriages between members of the same family-group or tribe; and, so far as appears at present, they could only have originated among endogamous tribes, or—in the case of marriage within the tribe—among tribes which allowed their members to marry among themselves or into other groups indifferently.

The form of marriage by gift, or that by sale and purchase, could never have originated with purely endogamous tribes. A tribe, in a primitive age, is just a group of kindred—more or less numerous, with common interests and possessions, where they have any other property besides their women; living together as an ungoverned fraternity, or under the headship of a pater-familias. Obviously within such a group there can be neither barter nor sale—neither the selling nor the buying of wives. On a marriage between two of its members, there is no foreign interest to be consulted or satisfied.

It is different if we conceive a number of such tribes aggregated in a political union to which the caste principle of its parts is extended; so that, while formerly the members of each could only marry among themselves, the members of all have acquired the right of intermarrying with one another. In form-

1. As the words endogamy and exogamy are new, an apology must be made for employing them. Instead of endogamy we might, after some explanations, have used the word caste. But caste connotes several ideas besides that on which we desire to fix attenion. On the other hand, the rule which declares the union of persons of the same blood to be incest has been hitherto unnamed, and it was convenient to give it a name. The words endogamy and exogamy (for which botanical science affords parallels) appear to be well suited to express the ideas which stood in need of names, and so we have ventured to use them, taking care in the text to make their meanings distinct.

ing this conception, we pass from marriages within the tribe to inter-tribal marriages. In an inter-tribal marriage one tribe loses a woman, the other acquires one; or, as sometimes happens, one loses a man, the other acquires one. In either case, there is room and a necessity for compensation. Such a marriage must be a subject of bargain, a matter of sale and purchase. And we may now perceive that the marriages of which coemptio may be taken as the civilised type, have their origin in intermarriages between distinct family groups or tribes.

But it is not in a primitive age, not until after a very considerable advance has been made in civility, that tribes are ever found joined in a political union. Such union indicates a state of friendliness between the tribes, brought about by common action for common objects. And should inter-tribal marriages come to be permitted among endogamous tribes, they could from the first be carried through by friendly negotiation. On the other hand, the degree of political union presupposed to explain the intermarriages must be such as to exclude the idea of the members of any tribe resorting to violence to obtain wives from any other. We conclude that, among this class of tribes, marriage by capture could have had no place. Still more certain is it that they could never come to form such an association between marriage and the act of rapine as would lead them to adopt the symbol of capture in marriage ceremonies; on the contrary, we should expect to find that they would, out of respect to immemorial usage in the case of marriages within the tribe, celebrate even their intertribal marriages—though really brought about by sale and purchase—by such ceremonies as had been customary among them in marriages between members of the tribe. And if the symbol of capture be ever found in the marriage ceremonies of an endogamous tribe, we may be sure that it is a relic of an early time at which the tribe was organised on another principle than that of endogamy.

And now let us postulate the existence of tribes, organised on what we shall call, for the want of a better name, the principle of exogamy—that is, which *prohibited marriage within the tribe*—and whose tribesmen were thus dependent on other

23

tribes for their wives. It is obvious that inter-tribal marriages could only be peaceably arranged between tribes whose relations were friendly. But peace and friendship were unknown between separate groups or tribes in early times, except when they were forced to unite against common enemies. The sections of the same family—when it fell into sections—became enemies by the mere fact of separation. And while this state of enmity lasted, exogamous tribes never could get wives except by theft or force.

If it can be shown, firstly, that exogamous tribes exist, or have existed; and secondly, that in rude times the relations of separate tribes are uniformly, or almost uniformly, hostile, we have found a set of circumstances in which men could get wives only by capturing them—a social condition in which capture would be the necessary preliminary to marriage. And if it be shown in a reasonable number of well-authenticated cases that these conditions—exogamy as tribal law, and hostility as the prevailing relation of separate tribes towards each other—exist or have existed, accompanied, as might have been expected, by a system of capturing wives, we shall be justified in concluding—failing the appearance of any phenomena inconsistent with such an explanation—that the same conditions have existed in every case where the system of capture prevailed, or where the form of capture has been observed as a ceremony of marriage. Nothing more than this is necessary to satisfy the conditions of a sound hypothesis.

We are in a position to do this and more. We shall be able to point to many tribes which habitually capture or captured their wives from foreign tribes; to show that exogamy is or was the law of these tribes; also, that there are cases of exogamous tribes whose tribesmen, marrying women by compact, always go through the form of capturing such women; that in all the modern instances where the symbol of capture is best marked, marriage within the tribe is prohibited as incestuous. We shall also find various circumstances common to exogamous tribes, and traceable in their case to the principle of exogamy, appearing more or less marked in the case of historical tribes

24

which have used the form of capture, supporting the conclusion that such tribes had once been exogamous.

It may easily be conceived how, among exogamous tribes, out of respect to immemorial usage, when friendly relations came to be established between tribes and families, and their members intermarried by purchase instead of capture, the form of invasion and capture should become an essential ceremony at weddings. It was unheard of from the remotest times that a woman became a man's wife except through being made his captive, forced or stolen away from her friends by him or for him. Surely something shall be wanting if there is not at least the appearance of a capture! So the Roman youths rush in with drawn swords, and feign to enact a tragedy; so the Kalmuck girl rides, as if for life, from her lord and master by prearrangement!

We now proceed to treat of the matter, in order, under the three following heads:—Firstly, The prevalence of capturing wives *de facto*; secondly, Whether, where that practice prevails, marriage between members of the same family-group, clan, or tribe, is forbidden, and the prevalence of that limitation of the right of marriage; and, thirdly, How far the state of war prevails among primitive groups?

4

On the Prevalence of the Practice of Capturing Wives, de facto

THE tribes amongst which prevails or has prevailed, the practice of getting wives by theft or force, are both numerous and widely distributed. We shall find them in America, in Australia, in New Zealand, in many of the islands of the Pacific, and in various parts of Asia and Europe.

It is among the tribes of American Indians that the practice is to be found in the greatest perfection. In particular, we find it fully displayed on the Orinoco, on the Amazons, everywhere in fact, from the Caribbean Sea to Cape Horn. The abject Fuegians, as we have seen,[1] have the practice in a modified or symbolised form in the marriages of men and women belonging to groups at peace with one another. But they have the reality as well as the fiction. Between many of their tribes there is a chronic state of war. "*Strangers*," reported Jemmy Button to Captain Fitzroy on one occasion,[2] "had been there, with whom he and his people had 'very much jaw;' they fought, threw 'great many stone,' and stole two women (in exchange for whom Jemmy's party stole one), but were obliged to retreat." The Horse Indians of Patagonia also, tribe against tribe, are commonly at war with one another, or with the Canoe Indians, the issues of victory in every case, being the capture of women and the slaughter of men. But the Oens or Coin-men would appear to be the most systematic of these savage marauders, for every year at the time of "red leaf" they are said to make excursions from the mountains in the north to plunder the Fuegians of their women, dogs, and arms.[3] Farther north still than the Oens men, we come successively on the tribes of the Amazons and of the Orinoco, all of which, excepting those reduced into missions, are continually at feud with one another,

1. See *ante*, pp. 18–19.
2. "Voyages of Adventure and Beagle," *ut supra*, vol. ii., p. 224.
3. *Idem*, p. 205.

and in turns rich in women or impoverished; feelings of mutual hate and the desire for means of subsistence being concurring causes of war. Of the tribes on the Amazons the accounts are not very distinct; but the habits of the Manaos in the Rio Negro district—which, as reported by Mr Bates,[4] are similar to those of the Coin-men—may be assumed not to be exceptional. There is no doubt, however, that the primitive habits of most of the Indian tribes have been much changed by the slave-hunting expeditions, at one time fostered by the Dutch and Portuguese. On slave-hunting being introduced in America, as in Africa, a market was found for captives of both sexes, and men as well as women became spoils of victory. No argument is needed to show that when women are systematically captured as in the above cited cases, they are captured with a view to the raising of children—in fact, with a view to their performing the part of wives. The fulness of the idea of a wife, according to our conceptions, is not, we need scarcely say, to be looked for amongst such savages. That idea can nowhere be fully realised till the circumstances of a people enable men and women to enjoy, or at least to look forward with confidence, to a permanent consortship.

Of the tribes of the great Caribbean nation we have happily a pretty full account from the pen of Alexander Von Humboldt.[5] The Caribbees fall into small tribes or family groups, often not numbering more than from 40 to 50 persons; Humboldt, indeed, takes frequent occasion to say that an Indian tribe is no more than a family. Where groups break up into sections, as they tend to do, and live apart from one another, the sections are found, though of one blood, and originally of one language, soon to speak dialects so different that they cannot understand one another. Become strangers, they are enemies except when forced to unite to make common cause against some powerful tribe which has proved a scourge to them all; enemies, and being at least at the time when Hum-

4. "The Naturalist on the Amazons." Second Edition, 1864, p. 199.
5. "Personal Narrative of Travels, etc." (1826). The passages bearing on the capturing of women among the tribes of the Orinoco, from which our account is taken, will be found at vol. v., pp. 210, 293, 422, 425, 548, 565; vol. vi., pp. 20, 21, 26; vol. vii., p. 449.

boldt wrote, cannibals, not only disposed to slay but to eat one another. In their wars, we may imagine, that while their male captives furnished means of subsistence, the women were preserved to be wives and luxuries.[6] To such an extent, indeed, did all the tribes of the Caribbean nation practise the capture of women—depend on aggression for their wives—that the women of any tribe were found to belong to different tribes, and to tribes of other nations, and that to such an extent, that nowhere were the men and women of the Caribbean race found to speak in one tongue.

Going northwards—to the wild Indians everywhere, as far as we follow them, the same account is applicable in varying degrees. It would indeed be misleading to omit to notice that in both North and South America tribes are to be found occupying much more elevated platforms of civility than those to which, for obvious reasons, we have given our attention. As among friendly groups of the Fuegians we find marriages of consent and of purchase (by labour commonly),[7] so also among friendly Patagonians; so also with the nations of the Huron tongue and the Attakapas, among whom the position of the women is exceedingly good. Indeed, all the processes have been going on through which every species of marriage would in time be developed. Even the red men of America are far from being primitive. A *really* primitive people in fact exists nowhere. For many thousands of years now, the various races of men have been in the school of experience, all making progress therein, though under different masters and in different forms. Hereafter we shall see how the old law of the red men, and of the natives of Australia, which counts blood relationship through females only, operates as an agent of civilization, and tends to supersede the barbarous practices of early savagery, and especially to obviate the necessity of capturing wives.

The capture of women for wives is found to prevail among the aborigines of the Deccan,[8] and in Affghanistan.[9] It pre-

6. Compare Erskine's "Pacific," p. 425 (1863).
7. See *ante*, pp. 18–19.
8. Colonel Walter Campbell's "Indian Journal," 1864, p. 400.
9. "Latham's Descriptive Ethnology." Vol. ii., p. 215.

vailed, according to Olaus Magnus, in Muscovy, Lithuania, and Livonia.[10] The form which it assumed among the peoples last named, so closely resembled what Kames describes as the custom among the Welsh, that we must quote the Archbishop's account of it:—

> Quicunque enim paganorum, sive rusticorum, filius suus uxorem ut ducat in animo habet, agnatos, cognatos, caeterosque vicinos in unum convocat, illisque talem isto in pago puellam nubilem versari, quam rapi, et suo filio in conjugem adduci proponit: hicommodum ad hoc tempus expectantes, ac tunc armati, equites suo more unius ad aedes conveniunt, posteaque ad eam rapiendam proficiscuntur. Puella autem quoad matrimonii contradictionem libera, ex insidiis opera exploratorum ubi moretur per eos direpta, plurimum eiulando opem consanguineorum amicorumque ad se liberandam implorat: quod si consanguinei vicinique clamorem istum exaudierunt, ipso momento armati adcurrunt, atque pro ea liberanda proelium committunt ut qui victores ista in pugna extiterunt his puella cedat.

The difference between the Welsh and the Muscovite practice lay in this, that in Wales, in the celebration of the marriage, betrothal came first, and the (sham) fight afterwards; while among the Muscovites an actual invasion came first, and if the bridegroom's party succeeded in carrying off the lady, there followed the consent of parents and the sponsalia:—

> Nec ante completam hanc celebritatem mutua carnali copula, pacto parentum interveniente, se commiscere solent conjungendi; quia immane cunctis gentibus crimen apparere dignoscitur si ante sponsalia sacra stupri illecebris virgo temeratur; immo summoperé cavent puellae ne copulam anticepent quia perpetuam cum prole sic suscepta infamiam luent.[11]

The intervention of the sponsalia and consent of parents before the consummation of the marriage, marks this as a transitional

10. "Historia de Gentibus Septentrionalibus." Book xiv., cap. ix., p. 481. Romae, 1555.
11. "Olaus Magnus," *ut supra*, p. 482.

form of the practice. But it is none the less a case of actual capture. Another advance and the sponsalia will precede the capture, and the fight be a farce.

According to Seignior Gaya,[12] this transitional form of the practice prevailed in his time in Poland, parts of Prussia, Samogithia and Lithuania. A lad's father having found where a girl lived, who would make a suitable wife for his son, he assembled his kindred and carried the lady off, after which application was made to her father for consent to complete the marriage.

There is ample reason to believe that the practice was general among the nations in the north of Europe and Asia. Olaus Magnus,[13] indeed, represents the tribes of the north as having been continually at war with one another either on account of stolen women, or with the object of stealing women, "propter raptas virgines aut arripiendas." His brother Johannes[14] dilates on the same topic, and mentions numerous cases in which the plunderers were of the royal houses of Denmark or Sweden. As did the kings, so did their subjects. Among the Scandinavians, before they became Christians, wives were almost invariably fought for and wedded at the sword-point. In Sweden, even long after the introduction of Christianity, women were often carried off when on the way to the church to be married. A wedding cortege was a party of armed men, and for greater security, marriages were generally celebrated at night. A pile of lances is said to be still preserved in the ancient church of Husaby in Gothland, into which were fitted torches; these weapons were borne by the groomsmen, and served the double purpose of giving light and protection.[15] Such a prevalence of lawlessness existing after the introduction of Christianity and comparative civilization, helps us to conceive what the habits of these people were in a more primitive age.

12. "Marriage Ceremonies," etc., *ut supra*, p. 35.
13. *Ut supra*, p. 328.
14. History of the Goths, Book xviii.; and see "Kames," *ut supra*, vol. i., p. 393.
15. "Book of Days," vol. i., p. 720. The groomsmen are said to have been called "best men" in the north from the strongest and stoutest of the bridegroom's friends being chosen for this duty.

We find capture *de facto* coexistent with capture as a form, and not unfrequent, among most of the rude tribes observing the form; its frequency depending partly on the degree of friendliness established between the tribes, and partly on the degree of fixity given by usage to the price to be paid for a bride. Where the parties cannot agree about the price, nothing is more common among the Kalmucks, Kirghiz, Nogais, and Circassians, than to carry the lady off by actual force of arms. The wooer having once got the lady into his yurt, she is his wife by the law, and peace is established by her relations coming to terms as to the price, after the thing has gone so far that they cannot help themselves. It is important to observe, that among these races the capture, though an irregular proceeding, makes marriage, even previous to terms being made between the capturer and the friends of the lady, and whether they are made or not.

That the practice of getting wives by capture *de facto*, prevails among the natives of Australia, is a fact familiar to most readers. It is not, however, *now* the sole or regular mode of getting a wife among the Australian tribes; and we do not claim to do more than show that there at present exists among them a practice of capturing wives so common as almost to be a system. And as we shall hereafter show that they are exogamous, and also that exogamous tribes which begin with a system of capturing wives, may progress—consistently with exogamy—to a system of betrothals, we shall ask the reader, conceding to us for the present that we shall be able to do so, to agree with us that so general a practice of capture, subsisting as it does among the Australians alongside of a system of betrothals, points unmistakeably to a previous stage when wives were usually captured.

Among the Australasians, according to one account,[16] when a man sees a woman whom he likes, he tells her to follow him, and when she refuses, he forces her to accompany him by blows, ending by knocking her down and carrying her off.[17]

16. See Appendix B, for an account of the practice among the Australian Blacks, which has appeared as this work was going through the press.

17. Turnbull, "Voyage Round the World," 1805. Vol. i., pp. 81, 82.

The same account (somewhat suspiciously) bears that this mode of courtship is rather relished by the ladies as a species of rough gallantry. The cases must indeed be rare in which a man finds a woman detached from her lord and protector, or the other members of her family; nor is it in human flesh and blood to take kicks and cuffs as compliments, in whatever spirit they may be administered. The following is the account given by Sir George Grey—a good authority:—"Even supposing a woman to give no encouragement to her admirers," he says,[18]

> many plots are always laid to carry her off, and in the encounters which result from these, she is almost certain to receive some violent injury, for each of the combatants orders her to follow him, and in the event of her refusing, throws a spear at her. The early life of a young woman at all celebrated for beauty is generally one continued series of captivity to different masters, of ghastly wounds, of wanderings in strange families, of rapid flights, of bad treatment from other females, amongst whom she is brought a stranger by her captor; and rarely do you see a form of unusual grace and elegance, but it is marked and scarred by the furrows of old wounds; and many a female thus wanders several hundred miles from the home of her infancy, being carried off successively to distant and more distant points.

As an Australian woman is always a wife, being betrothed after birth to some man of a different tribe or family-stock from her own, a stolen or captured wife is always stolen or taken from a prior husband. And as men do not readily part with their wives, and their tribesmen are bound to make common cause with them for the reparation of injuries, the capture of wives is a signal for war; and as the tribes have little property, except their weapons and their women, the women are at once the cause of war, and the spoils of victory.[19] The tribes, as might be expected, are exceedingly numerous, and exceed-

18. "Travels in North-Western Australia," 1841. Vol. ii., p. 249.
19. "Turnbull," *ut supra*, p. 82.

ingly small,[20] being a species of family groups, and, chiefly from the causes specified, they are continually at war with one another.[21] The reader may imagine the extent to which, among these myriad hordes of savages, the women are being knocked about, and the men accustomed to associate the acquisition of a wife with acts of violence and rapine.[22]

The native songs make frequent allusion to the practice of capturing wives. Here is the burden of one, sung by a heavy-hearted woman, upbraiding her lord, whose affections some recently acquired captive has drawn away from her,—

> Wherefore came you, Weerang,
> In my beauty's pride,
> Stealing cautiously,
> Like the tawny boreang,
> On an unwilling bride.
> 'Twas thus you stole me
> From one who loved me tenderly.
> A better man he was than thee,
> Who having forced me thus to wed,
> Now so oft deserts my bed.
> > Yang, yang, yang, yoh.
>
> Oh, where is he who won
> My youthful heart;
> Who oft used to bless
> And call me loved one:
> You, Weerang, tore apart
> From his fond caress
> Her whom you desert and shun;
> Out upon the faithless one!
> Oh, may the Boyl-yas bite and tear
> Her, whom you take your bed to share.
> > Yang, yang, yang, yoh.[23]

20. Sir George Grey says that the largest number of natives his party ever saw together, "numbered nearly two hundred, women and children included," *ut supra.* Vol. 1., p. 252.

21. Grey's "Travels," *ut supra.* Vol. 1., p. 256.

22. The reader will find, p. 318, vol. ii. of Grey's "Travels," a curious illustrative instance of the way in which a war about women may arise.

23. Grey's "Travels," vol. ii., p. 313.

Concerning the New Zealanders, it must suffice to say that the theft or capture of women plays a leading part in their popular legends, testifying to the prevalence of the practice, at least in their early history.[24] In New Zealand, and in the Feejee and other islands of the Pacific, the capture of wives appears to have been conjoined with cannibalism—the object of inter-tribal war being at once to procure women for wives and men for food, except in some districts where there was a special relish for the flesh of females.[25]

In the Institutes of Menu we have marriage by capture enumerated among "the eight forms of the nuptial ceremony used by the four classes." [26] It is the marriage called Racshasa, and is thus defined:—"The seizure of a maiden by force from her house while she weeps and calls for assistance, after her kinsmen and friends have been slain in battle or wounded, and their houses broken open, is the marriage called Racshasa.' Elsewhere[27] in the code it is mentioned as appropriated to the military class. "For a military man the before-mentioned marriages of Gandharvas and Racshases—whether separate or mixed, as when a girl is made captive by her lover, after a victory over her kinsmen—are permitted by law." The full scope and effect of this provision we shall have to consider hereafter. Meanwhile we notice that we have here the exact prototype of the Roman and Spartan forms, embalmed in a code of laws a thousand years before the commencement of our era; not as a form, but as living substance. This we hold to exclude any hypothesis except that which we are maintaining.[28]

We may notice, as further illustrating the subject, and as being in itself curious, that by the Mosaic Code the military class were, in defiance of the general law which declared that there was no connubium between Jews and Gentiles, allowed

24. "Polynesian Mythology, etc.," Sir George Grey, 1855, pp. 138, 147, 207, 235, 301.
25. Erskine's "Islands of the Western Pacific," and Jackson's "Narrative."
26. Chap. iii. 33 (Jones and Houghton).
27. Chap. iii. 26 (Jones and Houghton).
28. For the probable origin of the name Racshases, see Appendix B.

to take to wife women whom they captured in war, to whatever races they belonged. In Deut. xx. 10–14, the reader will find forms and regulations provided for the constitution of this species of marriage, and if interested to know the meaning of the rules, he will find a copious and learned discussion of them in the works of Selden.[29]

Thus far we have been dealing with facts. If we are right in our theory of the symbol of capture, it must be held that the Dorians, or at least some of the tribes composing the Spartan nation, and the Latins, or at least some of the tribes forming the commonalty of Rome, long had experience in the capturing of wives by force or stratagem. We leave to our Hellenists to consider how far the Doric legends may have new light thrown upon them by our view of the Spartan custom. How far, for instance, may the slaughter by Hercules of Eurylus and his sons, and the carrying away of Iole to be the wife of Hyllus— of Hyllus, who never occurs in mythology except in connection with the Dorians—be a mythical tradition of a rape of women from another tribe? How far may the genealogies of Doric heroes connected with the taking of Ephyra,—the capture of Astyocheia,—the feat of Hercules at Thespiae—the stories of Pluto and Proserpine, and of Boreas and Orithya—be but traditions of a quasi Caribbean prowess? It must be kept in mind, too, that the case cited from Herodotus in proof of the custom at Sparta is one of actual violence. At least, the lady was not carried off in terms of arrangement. Farther, to judge by what is reported of Theseus—even accepting the tradition as fabulous—we may conclude that the ancient Greeks generally were very lawless in this matter. To that hero's charge are laid numerous rapes of women whom he carried off to be his wives— his crimes of this description culminating in the seizure of Helen. Plutarch, indeed, in describing that affair, mentions a compact as having been entered into between Theseus and his companion in the seizure—Tyndarus—to the effect that he who should gain Helen by lot should have her to wife, but be

29. "De Jure Naturali et Gentium Juxta Disciplinam Ebraeorum." Lib. v., cap. xiii., fol. 617.

obliged to assist in procuring a wife for the other; which shows that these worthies trusted to their prowess to procure them wives.[30] As to the Romans—upon our theory—the story of the rape of the Sabines must be accepted as a mere mythical tradition of the ancient method of getting wives. The story, as might be expected, is reproduced in the traditions of many tribes, in many places, and in many forms. For instance, in the Irish Nennius[31] there is a tradition of such a rape of wives by the Picts from the Gael. In the very old poem, "The Cruithnians who propagated in the land of noble Alba," [32] the Irish are represented as giving three hundred wives to the Picts, on the condition that the succession to the crown among the Picts should always be through their females:—

> There were oaths imposed on them,
> By the stars, by the earth,
> That from the nobility of the mother
> Should always be the right to the sovereignty.

The story of the oaths is no doubt a fable to explain the descensus per umbilicum of the Picts. But, in "Duan Gircanash," [33] a poem on the origin of the Goedhel, reciting the same event, the Picts are represented as stealing the three hundred wives:—

> Cruithne, son of Cuig, took their women from them—
> It is directly stated—
> Except Tea, wife of Hermion,
> Son of Miledh.

30. There is no evidence that the Doric hordes who overran and established themselves in the Peloponnesus, were accompanied by their wives or children. It is most unlikely that they were so attended; and, except a surmise founded on the degree of influence enjoyed at a subsequent period by the women of Sparta, there is nothing in favour of the supposition. But that surmise proceeds on the ground that wives of a race alien to that of their husbands are not so likely to be well treated as they would be if they were of the same blood. Against this we must simply pronounce as being contrary to evidence.

31. Pp. 245–51.

32. Vv. 115–20. The Irish version of Nennius, 1848, p. 141.

33. Vv. 178–80, *ut supra*, p. 245.

And in consequence of the capture, the Gael, being left wife-less, had to form alliances with the aboriginal tribes of Ireland.

> There were no charming noble wives
>> For their young men,
> Their women having been stolen, they made alliance
>> With the Tuatha Dea.

We have the same story in the history of the Jews. Chapters xx and xxi of the Book of Judges contain highly instructive matter on this point, in a story, which, though laid in the time of the Judges, we must hold to be of very old date—a Jewish tradition belonging to the earliest history of Israel. The women of the tribe of Benjamin had been destroyed, and certain of the tribes of Israel had sworn not to give their daughters as wives to the men of Benjamin, who again could not take wives to themselves from the Gentiles, as by law they could marry only into one or other of the tribes of Israel. The difficulty of procuring wives for Benjamin—which Israel made its *own* difficulty—was solved by the wholesale slaughter of the inhabitants of Jabez-Gilead, whose population yielded 400 virgins: and next by the men of Benjamin enacting a rape of the Sabines for themselves, each man seizing and carrying off one of the daughters of Shiloh to be his wife, on an occasion when the women met for a festival in certain vineyards near Bethel.[34]

We can now say we have found the capture of women very extensively practised; and there can be no doubt that in most of the cases cited, the women captured were kept to be used as wives. In a number of well-marked cases we have found a system of capture—in the case of the Caribbean tribes of America, a system so general, that the women of a tribe were

34. See *Smith's Bible Dictionary*—Art. MARRIAGE—where it is remarked, that the phrase in the Old Testament (*e.g.*, Num. xii. 1; 1 Chron. ii. 21), "taking a wife," would seem to require to be taken in its literal meaning in the run of cases; "the taking" being the chief ceremony in the constitution of marriage. If the writer of that article is correct, we must believe that the Jews observed the *form* of capture, for in many cases where the phrase occurs we know the marriages were preceded by contracts.

commonly not only not of the same tribe with the men, but did not even speak the same language. We have seen among tribes in a transition state, in some cases, capture almost systematically practised, alongside of more civilized institutions; and in other cases, the practice of capture in various stages of progress towards a symbolism. We have seen the marriage by capture embodied in the code of India as an institution in favour of the only class which could be benefited by it—the warrior class; and no argument is needed to show that such a rule must have been a generalisation founded upon practice. A similar rule subsisted in favour of warriors among the Israelites. The former of these cases is, perhaps, chiefly valuable as presenting in a distinct shape the ante-type of the form of capture—a description of marriage by an actual capture so vividly recalling incidents of fictitious capture, as practised at Rome and elsewhere, as (in our opinion) to set at rest the question in what way the fiction originated. The latter case shows a provision made for marriage with foreign women, if captured, among tribes which, in no other case, allowed of marriage with foreign women; a provision indicating a very remarkable association between capture and marriage. It is not easy to believe that such a regulation, existing among endogamous tribes, is referable to the feeling that a victorious warrior should have the full disposal of spoils of war; it is much more likely that it was a relic of a time when the tribes —or rather the race from which they sprung—were not endogamous; and, if so, it carries us back to a remote antiquity when marriage and prowess in war were closely associated. We have seen that the mythic legends of various races, of which hitherto no rational explanation has been given, can, with great appearance of probability, be referred to the existence amongst such races in ancient times of a systematic capture of wives.

Farther research, and the observation of tribes hitherto unreported upon—at present we have not been able to say anything that would be satisfactory of the races of the continent of Africa[35]—will, we confidently expect, afford much additional

35. See Appendix B.

evidence of the prevalence of this practice. But we have done enough to entitle us to affirm that there has existed amongst various races of mankind *a system* of capturing women for wives.

5

*Of the Rule against Marriage between
Members of the Same Tribe—Of
the Coincidence of This Rule with
the Practice of Capturing Wives
de facto, and with the Form of
Capture in Marriage Ceremonies*

WE proceed to show the prevalence of the rule forbidding
marriage within the tribe or group of kindred, and the
concurrence of this ban with the fact or pretence of capturing
wives.

Here, still more than in our former investigation, we are
made to feel how imperfect and unconnected is the record
from which our facts have to be drawn; and farther, how
difficult it is to bring together such facts as have been observed, owing to the wide field over which they lie sparsely
scattered. In many cases, the authorities are silent just on the
points on which we are most eager for information; while on
matters of no moment they enlarge *ad nauseam*. But, too
often, they have nothing to tell. Skirting a coastline the
traveller sees natives at points here and there, and can describe
their dress and personal appearance; of their habits he is as
ignorant as a child of the free life of the beasts he sees in a
caravan. Where the opportunities of observation are better, the
observer often does not know what to look for. Of the *jus
connubii* among the Kalmucks not one word is said by Clarke
or Pallas or Strahlenberg! and but for some remarks of Bergmann's we should be entirely in the dark on the subject.

We begin with the Khonds. This people presents us with
capture *as a form*. Major-General Campbell says that the
Khonds marry women from remote places, the reason of which
he takes to be, that they have to buy their wives, and can get
them at lower prices at a distance. "They pretend, moreover,"

he adds,[1] "to regard it as degrading to bestow their daughters in marriage on men of their own tribe; and consider it more manly to seek their wives in a distant country." Major Mac-Pherson—a more intelligent witness—gives us the distinct statement, that among the Khonds intermarriage between persons of the same tribe, however large or scattered, is considered incestuous, and punishable by death;[2] a view more consistent with other known facts than that of General Campbell. "Marriage," Major MacPherson tells us,

> can take place only betwixt members of different tribes, and not *even with strangers who have been long adopted into or domesticated with a tribe,* and a state of war or peace appears to make little difference as to the practice of intermarriage between tribes. The people of Bara Mootah and of Burra Des, in Goomsur, have been at war time out of mind, and annually engage in fierce conflicts, but they intermarry every day. The women of each tribe, after a fight, visit each other to condole on the loss of their nearest common relations.

No doubt these friendly intermarriages must in time alter the relations of the tribes to one another; no doubt also the time was when the marriages were *not* effected in friendly fashion.

Let us now examine the cases of the Kalmucks and Circassians. To understand that of the former, we must attend a little to their political system. The Kalmucks are divided into four great nations or tribes under hereditary chiefs or khans;—the Khoskots, the Dzungars, the Derbets, and the Torgots. Each of these, according to Pallas,[3] is under the command of many little and nearly independent princes, called Noïons. The horde commanded by a Noïon is called an Oulouss, and is subdivided into several Aïmaks, each of which again is commanded by a noble called Saïssang. The Aïmaks again are subdivided into

---

1. *Ut supra,* p. 141.
2. "An Account of the Religion of the Khonds in Orissa," p. 57; and see MacPherson's Report on the Khonds, already referred to.
3. "Voyages dans Plusieurs Provinces de l'Empire de Russie, etc.," Paris (no date), vol. ii., p. 191. Nouvelle Edition.

many companies or khatoun, consisting of from ten to twelve tents, for convenience in pasturing; and each khatoun has its chief, but whether of the noble class we are not informed. It will thus be seen that there is among the Kalmucks a very large governing or princely class. Now, it appears that they have two systems of marriage law; one for the common people, and one for the nobles, or princely class. The common people, we are told by Bergmann,[4] enter into no unions in which the parties are not distant from one another by three or four degrees; but how the degrees are counted we are not informed. We are told that they have great abhorrence for the marriages of near relatives, and have a proverb—"The great folk and dogs know no relationship"—which Bergmann says is due to members of the princely class sometimes marrying sisters-in-law. We find, however, that these sisters-in-law are uniformly women of an entirely different stock from their husbands— different, or what is taken for different. For no man of the princely class (and it is in the marriages of the Kalmucks of this class, according to De Hell, that the form of capture is chiefly observed),[5] in any of the tribes, can marry a woman of his own tribe or nation. Not only must his wife be a noble, but she must be a noble of a different stock. For princely marriages, says Bergmann, "the bride is chosen from another people's stock—among the Derbets from the Torgot stock; and among the Torgots from the Derbet stock; and so on." Here, then, we have the principle of exogamy in full force in regard to the marriages of the governing classes—a large body in each nation, as we have seen, and, which is most to our present purpose, the body in whose marriages the form of capture is said to be observed. Whether or not the commonalty, with whom the nobles have no intermarriage—the people of black birth, as they are called—were originally of an alien, inferior, and conquered race; and whether or not the governing classes were originally independent exogamous tribes, we have the prohibition against marriage within the stock here concurrent with the form of capture in the weddings of the nobility. How

4. Bergmann's "Streiferein." Riga, 1804, vol. iii., p. 145, *et seq.*
5. See *ante*, p. 15.

far the commonalty observe the form we have no information, but it is not unlikely that they mimic, after a fashion, the marriage ceremonies of their superiors.

The case of the Circassians is simple, and quickly told:— "The Circassian word for their societies or fraternities," says Bell,[6]

> is "tleûsh," which signifies also "seeds." The tradition with regard to them is, that the members of each all sprang from the same stock or ancestry; and thus they may be considered as so many septs or clans, with this peculiarity, that, like seeds, all are considered equal. These cousins-german, or members of the same fraternity, are not only themselves interdicted from intermarrying, but their serfs, too, must wed with the serfs of another fraternity; and where, as is generally the case, many fraternities enter into one general bond, this law in regard to marriage must be observed by all. The confidential dependant, or steward, of our host here is a tokao who fled to his protection from Notwhatsh, because, having fallen in love with and married a woman of his own fraternity, he had become liable to punishment for this infraction of Circassian law. Yet his fraternity contained perhaps several thousand members. Formerly, such a marriage was looked upon as incest, and punished by drowning; now a fine of two hundred oxen, and the restitution of the wife to her parents, only are exacted.

Elsewhere,[7] Bell observes that these fraternities sometimes embrace thousands of persons, between whom marriage is by this ancient law totally prohibited. Here, too, as in Khondistan, and among the Kalmucks, we find the form of capture as well as the principle of exogamy.

Our next case is that of the Yurak Samoyeds (Siberia) among whom no man can take a wife from the tribe to which he belongs.[8] These Samoyeds hold kinsmanship to be coextensive with the tribe. All the members of the tribe, however

6. James Stanislaus Bell. "Journal of a Residence in Circassia," 1840, vol. 1., p. 347.

7. *Ut supra*, vol. ii., 110.

8. Latham, "Descriptive Ethnology," vol. ii. p. 455.

large or small, consider themselves relations, even where the common ancestor is unknown, and the evidence of consanguinity is wholly wanting. They fall into three divisions; the members of any of which may take wives from either of the other two, but not from their own; and as these divisions occupy sites far removed from one another, the Samoyeds have to go great distances for their wives.

We find the same state of things among the Kafirs, the Sodhas of northern India, the Beduanda Kallung (Singapore), and many others, including the Kirghiz and the Nogais.[9]

The Warali (India) tribes fall into divisions, and no man may marry a woman of his own division; he must go for a wife to one of the others. The Magar tribes fall into thums, all the members of each of which are supposed to be descended from a common ancestor: the Magar husband and wife must belong to different thums; within one and the same thum there is no marriage. Latham, in noticing the Magars, says—"This is the first time[10] I have found occasion to mention this practice. It will not be the last; on the contrary, the principle it suggests is so common as to be almost universal. We find it in Australia, in North and South America, in Africa, in Europe; we shall suspect and infer it in many places where the actual evidence of its existence is incomplete." This is a sweeping statement; but before we conclude we hope to show that it may fairly be accepted as correct.

In the Institutes of Menu it is laid down that a twice-born man might elect for nuptials "a woman not descended from his paternal or maternal ancestors within the sixth degree, and who is not known *by her family* name to be of the same primitive stock with his father." [11] This passage might be taken

9. It must not be thought that the form of capture occurs wherever exogamy prevails—that exogamy and the practice of capturing wives, which at a certain stage must be the resource of exogamous tribes, will in every case leave the form of capture behind them. We shall see the explanation of this hereafter. We have no information whether or not the Samoyeds practise the form of capture.

10. Vol. i. p. 80, "Descriptive Ethnology."

11. "Institutes of Menu," cap. iii., sec. 5. The words "or mother" occur in the gloss of Calluca. The rule fixing the stock by the father is, as we hope to show, far from being archaic. The twice-born classes are the

as a text for the discussion of the whole question of prohibited marriages, and we must dwell upon it somewhat, as it has an important bearing on the present investigation. The object of the rule is to prevent marriages between members of the same primitive stock; and it points out the family name as the test whether persons are of the same stock or not. It is as if a Fraser might not marry a Fraser, nor a M'Intosh a M'Intosh. By comparing the former state of the Highlands of Scotland with their present condition, especially with the condition of the town populations, we may clear our ideas regarding the origin, meaning, and effect of this institution. Of old each clan inhabited its particular strath or glen, and had its own well-defined hill ranges. In the Aird district there were none but Frasers; about Moy were none but M'Intoshes. The members of the clans are now interfused even in the country districts, and in towns like Inverness or Dingwall may be found members of all the clans. Now, suppose that originally a man was not allowed to marry a woman of his own clan, and that, subsequent to the interfusion of the clans, that ancient prejudice remained; the rule for enforcing it—the question of degrees of affinity apart—would just be the rule of Menu. So, in considering the origin of that rule, are we not remanded from the social state in which it was fixed in a code, to an earlier state, in which the population consisted of distinct clans or tribes organised on the principle of exogamy, and living apart from one another, as all tribes do in early times, until they are brought, by conquest or otherwise, under a common government? We have already had examples of tribes with this rule, so that, in this conception of the early state of the Indian population, we are making no improbable supposition. On the contrary, it is not only probable in itself, but it is the only supposition that will explain the fact; and if we accept it as indicating the

sacerdotal, military, and commercial (Menu x. 4). Nearly all the Indian castes are now divided into nations that do not intermarry; the nations into sects, some of which do not intermarry. All the nations are divided into certain families, called *gotrams*; a man cannot marry a woman of his own *gotram*. Buchanan's "Journey from Madras," 1807, vol. i. pp. 273, 300, 354, 396, 419, 421, 423; Muir's "Sanskrit Texts," Part II., 1859, pp. 378, 387; "Vivada Chintamani," Calcutta, 1863, Preface, p. 45.

origin of the rule of Menu, it gives us such an idea of the prevalence of this law of incest as we could never reach by the contemplation of the individual tribes among which it is the law. It will be recollected that the form of capture is found among the Hindus.[12]

We believe it may still be possible, in the case of some communities in which marriage between persons of the same family name is prohibited, to analyse the population into its constituent (stock) tribes, and to prove that the tribes had this law of incest. In one case, in particular, investigation seems to be courted. The Munnieporees, and the following tribes inhabiting the hills round Munniepore—the Koupooees, the Mows, the Murams, and the Murring—are each and all divided into four families—Koomul, Looang, Angom, and Ningthajà. A member of any of these families may marry a member of any other, but the intermarriage of members of the same family is strictly prohibited. In explanation, so far, of these family divisions,[13] we have the fact, well authenticated in the history of Munniepore, that the Koomul and Looang formerly existed as distinct and powerful tribes, and that the Koomul, in particular, at one time preponderated in the valley. Presuming that these tribes held intermarriages of their members to be incestuous, the origin of two of the family divisions, and of the marriage law, is plain enough, at least so far as the hill tribes are concerned; and it is in the hills alone that the law is strictly enforced. Most of the members of the tribes would remain in the valley and mix with the Meithei, by whose prowess they were vanquished; but we can conceive that bands of the Koomul and Looang might escape to the hills, and mix with each other and with the tribes of the Angom and Ningthajà, whose existence in former times we must postulate, in explanation of the family divisions of the same names. Is it beyond hope that the farther examination of local traditions, or exploration of the wilds to the south and north-east of Munniepore, may yet furnish us with information regarding

12. *Ante,* p. 14, and see Appendix A.
13. "Account of the Valley of Munnipore and of the Hill Tribes." McCulloch, 1859, pp. 49–69.

the Angom and Ningthajà, or with data from which their existence in former times may be legitimately inferred, apart from the present speculation?

The conclusion at which we have arrived as to the origin of the rule of Menu, will also explain the case of the native populations of Australia, North and South America, and the islands in the Pacific. In these quarters we obtain light regarding the causes which lead to the break up of the primitive exogamous groups, and to the intermixture in local tribes of people recognised as being of different bloods. Let us first attend to the Australians, whom we find divided into small tribes named after the districts which they inhabit; for though they are nomads, their wanderings, like those of the nomadic agriculturists of the Indian hills, are circumscribed within well-defined bounds. It appears that the tribe inhabiting a particular district regards itself as the owner thereof, and the intrusion of any other tribe upon that district as an invasion to be resented and punished; and that within the district individuals have portions of land appropriated to them.[14] Thus the tribal system is in force, with an apparent perfect separation and independence of the tribes. But, on close examination, the tribes are found to be fused and welded together by blood-ties in the most extraordinary manner. According to credible accounts,[15] the natives of different tribes extending over a great portion of the continent, are divided into a few families, and all the members of a family, in whatever local tribes they may be, bear the same name as a second or family name. These family names and divisions are perpetuated and spread throughout the country by the operation of two laws: first, that the children of either sex always take the name of the mother; and second, that a man cannot marry a woman of his own family name. The members of these families, though scattered over the country, are yet to some intents as much united as if they formed separate and independent tribes; in particular, the members of each family are bound to unite for the purposes

14. Letter, Dr. Lang to Dr. Hodgkin, 1840. "Reports of the Aboriginal Protection Society.
15. Grey's "Journals," etc., vol. ii., chap. xi.

of defence and vengeance, the consequence being that every quarrel which arises between the tribes is a signal for so many young men to leave the tribes in which they were born, and occupy new hunting grounds, or ally themselves with tribes in which the families of their mothers may happen to be strong, or which contain their own and their mother's nearest relatives. This *secession*, if we may so call it, is not always possible, but it is of frequent occurrence notwithstanding; where it is impossible, the presence of so many *of the enemy* within the camp affords ready means of satisfying the call for vengeance; it being immaterial, according to the native code, by whose blood the blood-feud is satisfied, provided it be blood of the offender's kindred. Thus, as the Australians are polygamists, and a man often has wives belonging to different families, it is not in quarrels uncommon to find children of the same father arranged against one another; or, indeed, against their father himself, for by their peculiar law the father can never be a relative of his children.[16] Among the Kamilaroi, a numer-

16. Mr. Maine has been unable to conceive how human beings could be grouped on any principle more primitive than that of the patriarchal system, or be bound together by any ruder blood-ties than those of agnation derived from the patria potestas. We think his mistake has arisen from a too exclusive attention, in his researches, to those systems of ancient law which, like the Hindoo, Roman, and Jewish, belonged to races which were far advanced at the earliest dates to which their history goes back. Had he examined the primitive races now extant, he certainly would not have written the following passage ("Ancient Law," 1861, p. 149): "It is obvious that the organisation of primitive societies would have been confounded if men had called themselves relatives of their mother's relatives. The inference would have been that a person might be subject to two distinct patriae potestates; but distinct patriae potestates implied distinct jurisdictions, so that anybody amenable to two of them at the same time would have lived under two dispensations. As long as the family was an imperium in imperio, a community within the commonwealth, governed by its own institutions, of which the parent was the source, the limitation of relationship to the agnates was a necessary security against a conflict of laws in the domestic forum." Here we see the ingenious thinker trammelled by notions derived from Roman jurisprudence. Among the Australian Blacks—to confine ourselves to a single instance—we have seen that men are relatives of their mother's relatives, and of none other; and that their societies are, *aliunde*, held together, notwithstanding the conflict of laws in the domestic forum, engendered by polygamy, exogamy, and female kinship. Kinship depends, in fact,

ous tribe residing to the north-west of Sidney, the rules in force are very complex and peculiar. These tribesmen fall into divisions resembling castes, and at the same time observe the rule against marriages between members of the same family.[17]

Our information is so imperfect that we do not know whether there exist anywhere in Australia tribes whose distinctive names are those of the families into which the population is divided. But we should not expect to find such tribes. The constant tendency of groups to fall to pieces, and of the parts to separation and independence of one another, and the practice of naming groups from their lands, would tend to obliterate the traces of the original stock-groups, except so far as they have been preserved in the names of families to keep the blood pure by avoidance of marriage between members of the same stock. But we cannot doubt that such stock-groups at one time existed, organised on the principle of exogamy, and were the germs of the native population. Whencesoever they were derived, it was inevitable, that the law which recognised blood relationship as existing only through females, conspiring with the primitive instinct of the race against marriage between members of the same stock, should tend in the process of time to transfuse the blood of each stock through all the tribal divisions. The men of the group A marrying women of the group B; and the men of the group B marrying women of the group A; and all the children of the women of B being counted of the stock of B; and all the children of the women of A being counted of the stock of A; we at once have so many B's within A, and so many A's within B. And so on, until in time A's from the northmost point appear in the homes of Z at the southmost; and Z's in the homes of A. Each local tribe would thus contain within itself members between whom there was connubium; the original tribal divisions would be lost sight of, and

---

not at all on convenience. The first kinship is the first possible—that through mothers, about whose parental relation to children there can be no mistake. And the system of kinship through mothers only, operates to throw difficulties in the way of the rise of the patria potestas, and of the system of agnation. But of this hereafter.

17. Mr. Ridley's account quoted, p. 491, vol. ii., Prichard's "Natural History of Man." Norris' edition.

nothing would remain of the stock-groups but the family names to which they gave birth. Should the process of transfusion go far enough, the state of matters which would lead to the practice of capturing wives would be modified, but not extinct. The system of polygamy of itself, and any want of balance between the sexes of different families within a tribe, would long tend to maintain this practice; which, moreover, like every other practice connected with marriage or religion, must be credited with a special tenacity of existence. As we have seen, there prevails among the Australians a system of betrothals— always between persons of different stocks—along with an extensive practice of capturing wives. This is just what might be expected if our theory of the origin of capture be a sound one. Since the tribes of Australians, while exogamous in principle, contain persons who regard each other as of different descent and free to intermarry, marriage can be, and is, made the subject of bargain. Again, habits formed in previous times of necessity—and no doubt occasional necessity still existing— keep up the practice of capture.

We now take the case of the American Indians—North and South. They have political and district divisions;[18] but besides these the nations among them have had from time immemorial divisions into families or clans. "At present, or till very lately" —we quote from the Archaeologia Americana—

> every nation was divided into a number of clans, varying in the several nations from three to eight or ten, the members of which respectively were dispersed indiscriminately throughout the whole nation. It has been fully ascertained that the inviolable regulations by which these clans were perpetuated amongst the southern nations were, first, that no man could marry in his own clan; secondly, that every child should belong to his or her mother's clan. Among the Choctaws there are two great divisions, each of which is subdivided into four clans, and no man can marry in any of the four clans belonging to his division. The restriction among the Cherookees, the Creeks, and the Natches, does not ex-

18. "Archaeologia Americana," vol. ii. p. 109.

tend beyond the clan to which the man belongs. There are sufficient proofs that the same division into clans, commonly called tribes, exists among almost all the other primitive nations. But it is not so clear that they are subject to the same regulations which prevail amongst the southern Indians.

At the root of these divisions and prohibitions we find here, as in Australia, the feeling that marriage between persons of the same blood is incestuous. "They profess to consider it highly criminal for a man to marry a woman whose *totem* (family name) is the same as his own, and they relate instances when young men, for a violation of this rule, have been put to death by their own relatives." [19] The Indian nations, they say,

19. From a circular letter by Mr. L. H. Morgan of Rochester, New York, issued by the United States Government to its diplomatic agents and consuls in foreign countries, and which contains much interesting information regarding the laws of primitive relationship, we quote the following passage as the most recent and authoritative statement regarding the tribal divisions of the red men:—

"Nearly all, if not all, of the Indian Nations upon this continent were anciently subdivided into *Tribes* or *Families*. These tribes, with a few exceptions, were named after animals. Many of them are now thus subdivided. It is so with the Iroquois, Delawares, Iowas, Creeks, Mohaves, Wyandottes, Winnebagoes, Otoes, Kaws, Shawnees, Choctaws, Otawas, Ojibewas, Potowottomies, etc.

"The following tribes are known to exist, or to have existed in the several Indian Nations—the number ranging from three to eighteen in each: The Wolf, Bear, Beaver, Turtle, Deer, Snipe, Heron, Hawk, Crane, Duck, Loon, Turkey, Musk-rat, Sable, Pike, Cat-fish, Sturgeon, Carp, Buffalo, Elk, Rein-deer, Eagle, Hare, Rabbit, and Snake; also, the Reed-grass, Sand, Water, Rock, and Tobacco-plant.

"Among the Iroquois—and the rule is the same to the present day in most of the nations enumerated—no man is allowed to marry a woman of his own tribe, all the members of which are consanguinii. This was unquestionably the ancient law. It follows that husband and wife were always of different tribes. The children are of the tribe of the *mother*, in a majority of the nations; but the rule, if anciently universal, is not so at the present day. Where descent in the female line prevailed, it was followed by several important results, of which the most remarkable was the perpetual disinheritance of the male line. Since all titles as well as property descended in the female line, and were hereditary, in strictness, in the tribe itself, a son could never succeed to his father's title of Sachem, nor inherit even his medal or his tomahawk. If the Sachem, for example, was of the Wolf tribe, the title must remain in that tribe, and his son, who was necessarily of the tribe of his mother, would be out of

were divided into tribes just lest any one might, through temptation or accident, marry a near relation, which "at present is scarcely possible, for whoever intends to marry must take a person of a different tribe," [20] and the same feeling has been remarked by Dobrizhoffer in South America.[21]

What we have said of the Australians may be assumed to have been true, at one time at least, of the New Zealanders. In "The Curse of Mania" [22] and several other of the New Zealand legends we have evidence that the wife never belonged to the tribe of her husband, and that the children belonged to the family of their mother. So among the Feejees, who appear to count blood relationship through the mother only. In the system of vasu-ing, which determines the claims of children upon the tribe of their mother, we have evidence that the mother always belongs to a different tribe from the father, and that the children are held to be of the family or tribe of their mother.[23] At any rate, vasu-ing is a relic of a stage in the development of the Feejees wherein that was the rule.

Curiously enough, there is reason for believing that exogamy prevailed among the Picts; in other words, according to the most approved doctrine, among the Gael or Highlanders; which fact bears at once on the rapes of the Cruithnians, the old Welsh and French customs, and the plebeian marriage-ceremonies of Rome, for the Celtic element was strong in Rome. That the Celts were anciently lax in their morals, and rec-

---

the line of succession; but the brothers of the deceased Sachem would be of the Wolf tribe, being of the same mother, and so would the sons of his sisters: hence we find that the succession fell either upon a brother of the deceased ruler or upon a nephew. Between a brother of the deceased, and the son of a sister, there was no law establishing a preference: neither as between several brothers on one side, or several sisters on the other, was there any law of primogeniture. They were all equally eligible, and the law of election came in to decide between them."— *Cambrian Journal*, vol. iii., second series, p. 149.

20. Tanner's "Narrative," p. 313, quoted in Arch. Amer., and by Grey, *ut supra*.

21. "Account of the Abipones," vol. i. p. 69.

22. "Polynesian Mythology," *ut supra*, p. 162. In "The Curse of Mania" the reader will find an instance of children fleeing from the tribe of birth to that of the mother's kindred.

23. Erskine's "Pacific," *ut supra*, pp. 153–215.

ognised relationship through mothers only, are facts well vouched;[24] and of such facts it is the usual concomitant, that the children should be named after the mother. The facts brought out by the distinguished antiquary, Mr. Skene, from a study of the list of Pictish kings down to 731, when Bede says that the law of succession through females was still in force, may to some extent be explained by the sons taking the names of their mothers; but they point to something beyond this. By favour of Mr. Skene, we are at liberty to give here the results at which he has arrived, and which have not hitherto been published.

1st, That brothers always succeeded each other.

2d, That in no case does a son succeed a father; after the brothers have reigned a new family comes in.

3d, That the names of the fathers and of the sons are quite different. In no case does the name borne by any of the sons appear among the names of the fathers, nor conversely is there an instance of a father's name appearing among the sons.

4th, The names of the sons consist of a few Pictish names borne by sons of different fathers. These are—6 Drusts, 5 Talorgs, 3 Nectans, 2 Galans, 6 Gartnaidhs, 4 Brudes. In no case does the name of a father occur twice in the list of fathers.

5th, In the list there are two cases of sons bearing Pictish names whose fathers are known to have been strangers, and *these are the only fathers of whom we have any account.* They are—1. Talorg Macainfrit. His father was undoubtedly Ainfrit, son of Aethelfrith, King of Northumbria, who took refuge among the Picts, and afterwards became King of Northumbria; 2. Brude Mac Bile. His father was a Welshman, King of the Strath-Clyde Britons. In an old poem Brude Mac Bile is called son of the King of Ailcluaide, *i.e.,* Dumbarton; and when, by the battle of Drunichen, he became King of the Picts, another old poem says, "to-day Brude fights a battle about the land of his grandfather."

The fact that the only fathers of whom we have any account are known to have been strangers—especially when taken

24. Caesar, "De Bello Gallico," lib. v. § 14. Xiphilinus, Monum. Histor. lxi. Solinus, idem. Irish Nennius, liv.

along with the other facts which we possess about the Picts—raises a strong presumption that all the fathers were men of other tribes. At any rate there remains the fact, after every deduction has been made, that the fathers and mothers were in no case of the same family name.

We have now, by an irresistible array of instances, established the fact of exogamy being a most widely prevailing principle of marriage-law among primitive races. We have found the areas to be, for the chief part, conterminous within which exogamy and the practice of capturing wives *de facto* prevails. Farther, in all the modern instances in which the symbol of capture is most marked, we have found that marriage within the tribe is prohibited as incest, as among the Khonds, the Fuegians, the Kalmucks, and Circassians; also that in several cases where traces of the symbol appear, as among the Nogais and the Kirghiz, exogamy is more or less perfectly observed. We have seen good reason for thinking that exogamy and the practice of capture *de facto*, co-existed among the old Celts; and that in that co-existence lies the explanation of the symbol among the French, the Welsh, and the plebeians of Rome. Of the *jus connubii* of the Muscovites and Livonians in former times we have no direct information. Magnus is silent on the subject. But it is implied in his narrative that husband and wife invariably belonged to different kinships and village communities. We have found exogamy and the symbol co-existing in ancient India. Not to dwell on the slighter and more doubtful instances, we think it must now be admitted that we have sufficiently proved both the existence of exogamous tribes, and that among such tribes there prevails, or has prevailed, a system of capturing women for wives.

6

On the State of Hostility

THE state of hostility is a theme which requires no re-search to illustrate it. It is a fact too familiar to require demonstration. If war is a lamentable feature of human life, it is not quite so ugly among savages as when waged by civilized men. In proportion to their masses and the weight of the interests at stake, the advanced nations are perhaps quite as frequently embroiled as the most barbarous; also in their case the natural beneficence—if we may so call it—of the impulse to feud is not always apparent. In the lower stages of society we recognise war as a condition of the rise of govern-ments, of the subordination of classes, of civility—its agonies as the growing pains of civil society; in the higher it appears too often as a mere scourge of mankind, deforming and impair-ing, if not destroying, the precious results and accumulations of long periods of peace and industry.

If the wars of savages are petty, they are habitual. While the domestic affections are little pronounced, the social are confined to the smallest fraction of humanity. Whoever is foreign to a group is hostile to it. Even in comparatively ad-vanced stages of savagery, groups rarely combine for common purposes; when they do—the object of the combination being accomplished—they return to their isolated independence. And when tribes have combined in nations, and the nations have become polite, it is yet some time before a distinction is drawn between strangers and enemies. No wonder if the distinction be not made by savages. Whoever is not with them is against them—a rival in the competition for food, a possible plunderer of their camp and ravisher of their women. Lay out the map of the world, and wherever you find populations unrestrained by the strong hand of government there you will find perpetual feud, tribe against tribe, and family against family.

It would be superfluous to select particular districts from which to illustrate this truth, exemplifications of which we have already, in so many instances, had occasion to see. The state of hostility is the normal state of the race in early times. It is incidental to the separation and independence of men in small communities; and, while the arts are as yet in their infancy, small communities are a necessary result of the conditions of subsistence. Thus Lot separates from Abraham. Jacob goes one way and Esau goes another. And with separation comes estrangement—differences of language and habits—hostility. Till in a short time blood relations are as much apart—as foreign to one another—as people of different races and states.

7

Exogamy: Its Origin—Comparative Archaism of Exogamy and Endogamy

A T the outset of our argument it was seen that if it could be shown that exogamous tribes existed, and that the usual relations of savage tribes to each other were those of hostility, we should have found a social condition in which it was inevitable that wives should systematically be procured by capture. It also appeared that if the existence of exogamous tribes either actually capturing their wives, or observing the symbol of capture in their marriage ceremonies, should be established in a reasonable number of cases, it would be a legitimate inference that exogamy has prevailed wherever we find a system of capture, or the form of capture, existing. We now confidently submit that the conditions requisite for this inference have been amply established in the three preceding chapters; so that we may conclude that wherever capture, or the form of capture, prevails, or has prevailed, there prevails, or has prevailed, exogamy. Conversely, we may say that, wherever exogamy can be found, we may confidently expect to find, after due investigation, at least traces of a system of capture. We have traced the law and the corresponding practice among tribes scattered over a large portion of the globe. What farther knowledge of rude tribes now existing may show to us it would be idle to conjecture; but it might be plausibly maintained, upon the facts already known to us, that the principle of exogamy has in fact prevailed, and the system of capturing wives in fact been practised at a certain stage among every race of mankind.

Perhaps there is no question leading deeper into the foundations of civil society than that which regards the origin of exogamy, unless it be the cognate question of the origin of caste, which admits, however, more readily of ingenious surmises, and what mathematicians call singular solutions. We believe this restriction on marriage to be connected with the practice in early times of female infanticide, which, rendering women scarce, led at once to polyandry within the tribe, and the capturing of women from without. Female infanticide— common among savages everywhere—prevails as a system, and has been customary from time immemorial amongst many of the races that exhibit the symbol of capture.[1] With some of the exogamous races it appears to be the rule to kill all female children, except the first-born when a female. To tribes surrounded by enemies, and, unaided by art, contending with the difficulties of subsistence, sons were a source of strength, both for defence and in the quest for food, daughters a source of weakness. Hence the cruel custom which, leaving the primitive human hordes with very few young women of their own— occasionally with none[2]—and, in any case, seriously disturbing the balance of the sexes within the hordes, forced them to prey upon one another for wives. Usage, induced by necessity, would in time establish a prejudice among the tribes observing it—a prejudice strong as a principle of religion, as every prejudice relating to marriage is apt to be—against marrying women of their own stock. A survey of the facts of primitive life, and the breakdown of exogamy in advancing communities, exclude the notion that the law originated in any innate or primary feeling against marriage with kinsfolk. Indeed, we shall hereafter see that it is probable that necessity may have established the prejudice against marrying women of the group even before the facts of blood-relationship had made any deep impression on the human mind. At present it may be observed that the existence of infanticide, so wide-spread in itself, indicates how slight the strength of blood-ties was in primitive times. To form an adequate notion, on the other hand, of the extent to which tribes might, by means of infanticide, deprive

1. The Circassians have not the practice. But there is reason to believe that they only commenced sparing their daughters when they found a profitable market for them. For an explanation of the effect of the law of blood-feud on the practice of infanticide, see the end of chap. 8.

2. In one village of the Phweelongmai, on the eastern frontier of India, Colonel McCulloch found in 1849 that there was not a single female child.

themselves of their women, we have only to bear in mind the multitude of facts which testify to the thoughtlessness and improvidence of men during the childish stage of the human mind.

To show that the analysis by which the true solution of the questions respecting endogamy and exogamy is to be obtained, is the analysis of a series of phenomena which appears to form a progression, we notice the following as the divisions into which the less advanced portions of mankind fall when ranked according to their rules as to connubium:—

EXOGAMY PURE.—1. Tribal (or family) system.—Tribes separate. All the members of each tribe of the same blood, or feigning themselves to be so. Marriage prohibited between the members of the tribe.

2. Tribal system.—Tribe a congeries of family groups, falling into divisions, clans, thums, etc. No connubium between members of same division: connubium between all the divisions.

3. Tribal system.—Tribe a congeries of family groups embracing several village communities or nomadic hordes: members of families (or primitive stock groups) somewhat interfused. No connubium between persons whose family name points them out as being of the same stock.

4. Tribal system.—Tribe in divisions. No connubium between members of the same divisions: connubium between some of the divisions; only partial connubium between others —e.g., a man of one may marry a woman of another, but a woman of the former may not marry a man of the latter. Approach to caste.

5. Tribal system.—Tribe in divisions. No connubium between persons of the same stock: connubium between each division and some other. No connubium between some of the divisions. Caste.

ENDOGAMY PURE.—6. Tribal (or family) system.—Tribes separate. All the members of each tribe of the same blood, or feigning themselves to be so. Connubium between members of the tribe: marriage without the tribe forbidden and punished.

7. Tribal system indistinct.—Members of primitive (stock)

groups interfused. (1.) Marriage forbidden except between persons whose family name points them out as being of the same stock. (2.) Marriage forbidden except between the members of particular families. Persons having connubium marked as a caste, old tribal divisions being lost sight of.

Although these tribal systems may be arranged as above so as to *seem* to form a progression, of which the extremes are pure exogamy on the one hand, and endogamy—transmuted into caste of the Mantchu and Hindu types—on the other, we have at present no right to say that these systems were developed in anything like this order in tribal history. They may represent a progression from exogamy to endogamy, or from endogamy to exogamy; or the middle terms, so to speak, may have been produced by the combination of groups severally organised on the one and the other of these principles. The two types of organisation may be equally archaic. Men must originally have been free of any prejudice against marriage between relations—not necessarily endogamous, *i.e.*, forbidding marriage except between kindred, but still more given to such unions than to unions with strangers. From this primitive indifference they may have advanced, some to endogamy, some to exogamy.

The separate endogamous tribes are nearly as numerous, and they are in some respects as rude, as the separate exogamous tribes. It may be noted, however, that endogamy appears in populations formed by the fusion of many tribes, as the almost uniform characteristic of the dominant race. Hereafter we shall see how a tribe organised on the principle of endogamy might be developed from one organised on the principle of exogamy, in perfect consistency with the law against the intermarriage of relations. And while the existence of tribes like those of the Mantchu Tartars, who prohibit marriages between persons *whose family names are different*, is of great weight in favour of endogamy as a primitive type of organisation; on the other hand, castes like those of India, embracing members of several different families, and with a marriage law like that of Menu, strongly suggest that many endogamous tribes have been developed from tribes organised on the opposite principle. Since, moreover, the reconversion of a caste or of an endogamous tribe into an exogamous tribe is inconceivable—we have no experience of caste disappearing except in advanced communities, and then only on a revolution of sentiment being produced by political influences—the choice seems to be between regarding the two classes of tribes as organised *ab initio* on distinct principles, or holding the exogamous to be the more archaic.

We may notice as strange, that frequently tribes thus oppositely organised are found inhabiting the same area. On the sub-Himalayan ranges, for example, are the Sodhas, who intermarry with the Rajputs, not with each other; the Magars, who prohibit marriages between members of the same thum; and, again, the Kocch, Bodo, Ho, and Dhumal, who are forbidden to marry except to members of their own tribes or kiels. And, in some districts—as in the hills on the north-eastern frontier of India, in the Caucasus, and the hill ranges of Syria—we find a variety of tribes, proved, by physical characteristics and the affinities of language, of one and the same original stock, yet in this particular differing *toto coelo* from one another—some forbidding marriage within the tribe, and some proscribing marriage without it.

What has been said is enough to show that the question of the comparative archaism of exogamy and endogamy is as difficult as it is interesting. We shall in the next chapter lead up to a fuller discussion of that question, while investigating more minutely than we have hitherto done the conditions of the form of capture being evolved. We shall there endeavour to establish the following propositions:—1. That the most ancient system in which the idea of blood-relationship was embodied, was the system of kinship through females only. 2. That the primitive groups were, or were assumed to be, homogeneous. 3. That the system of kinship through females only tended to render the exogamous groups heterogeneous, and thus to supersede the system of capturing wives. 4. That in the advance from savagery the system of kinship through females only was succeeded by a system which acknowledged kinship through males also; and which, in most cases passed into a system which acknowledged kinship through males only. 5. That the system of kinship through males tended to rear up homogeneous groups, and thus to restore the original condition of affairs —where the exogamous prejudice survived—as regards both the practice of capturing wives and the evolution of the form of capture. 6. That a local tribe, under the combined influence of exogamy and the system of female kinship, might attain a balance of persons of different sexes regarded as being of different descent, and that thus its members might be able to intermarry with one another, and wholly within the tribe, consistently with the principle of exogamy. 7. That a local tribe, having reached this stage and grown proud through success in war, might decline intermarriage with other local tribes and become a caste. 8. That on kinship becoming agnatic, the members of such a tribe might yield to the universal tendency of rude races to eponomy, and feign themselves to be all derived from a common ancestor, and so become endogamous. And 9. That there is reason to think that some endogamous tribes became endogamous in this manner.

8

Ancient Systems of Kinship and Their Influence on the Structure of Primitive Groups

THE earliest human groups can have had no idea of kinship. We do not mean to say that there ever was a time when men were not bound together by a feeling of kindred. The filial and fraternal affections may be instinctive. They are obviously independent of any theory of kinship, its origin or consequences; they are distinct from the perception of the unity of blood upon which kinship depends; and they may have existed long before kinship became an object of thought. What we would say is, that ideas of kinship must be regarded as growths—must have *grown* like all other ideas related to matters primarily cognizable only by the senses; and that the fact of consanguinity must have long remained unperceived as other facts, quite as obvious, have done. In other words, at the root of kinship is a physical fact, which could be discerned only through observation and reflection—a fact, therefore, which must for a time have been overlooked. No advocate of innate ideas, we should imagine, will maintain their existence on a subject so concrete as relationship by blood.

A group of kindred in that stage of ignorance is the rudest that can be imagined. Though they were chiefly held together by the feeling of kindred, the *apparent* bond of fellowship between the members of such a group would be that they and theirs had always been companions in war or the chase—joint-tenants of the same cave or grove. To one another they would simply be as comrades. As distinguished from men of other groups, they would be of the group, and named after it.

Hence, most naturally, on the idea of blood-relationship arising, would be formed the conception of *Stocks*. Previously individuals had been affiliated not to persons, but to some group. The new idea of blood-relationship would more readily demonstrate the group to be composed of kindred than it would evolve a special system of blood-ties between certain of the individuals in the group. The members of a group would now have become brethren. As distinguished from men of other groups, they would be of the group-stock, and named after the group.[1]

The development of the idea of blood-relationship into a system of kinship, must have been a work of time—at least the establishment over any great area of any such system as an institution of customary law must have been slowly effected. It is most improbable that that idea, when first formed, was anywhere at once embodied in a well-defined system of kinship.

We shall endeavour to show—

I.—*That the most ancient system in which the idea of blood-relationship was embodied, was a system of kinship through females only.*

Once a man has perceived the fact of consanguinity in the simplest case—namely, that he has his mother's blood in his veins, he may quickly see that he is of the same blood with her other children. A little more reflection will enable him to see that he is of one blood with the brothers and sisters of his mother. On further thought he will perceive that he is of the same blood with the children of his mother's sister. And, in process of time, following the ties of blood through his mother, and females of the same blood, he must arrive at a system of kinship through females. The blood-ties through females being obvious and indisputable, the idea of blood-relationship, as soon as it was formed, must have begun to develop, however slowly, into a system embracing them. What further development this idea might have—whether it would simultaneously have a development in the direction of kinship through males— must have depended on the circumstances connected with

1. It is a question for philologists how far the earliest words which denote a human group involve the idea of blood. In one case they seem not to have done so. Grant, in his "Origin and Descent of the Gael," says that teadhloch and cuedichc or coedichc, Gaelic names for family, mean the first having a common residence; the second those who eat together. The Gael had, however, the more general terms finne and cinne—the former meaning born of the same stock, and the latter denoting the tribe.

paternity. If the paternity of a child were usually as indisputable as the maternity, we might expect to find kinship through males acknowledged soon after kinship through females.[2] But however natural it might be that men should think of blood-ties as possible to be propagated through fathers, blood-ties through fathers could not find a place in a system of kinship, unless circumstances usually allowed of some degree of certainty as to who the father of a child was, or of certainty as to the father's blood.[3] A system of relationship through fathers could only be formed—as we have seen that a system of relationship through mothers would be formed—after a good deal of reflection upon the fact of paternity. And fathers must usually be known before men will think of relationship through fathers—indeed, before the idea of a father can be formed. There could be no *system* of kinship through males if paternity was usually, or in a great proportion of cases, uncertain. The requisite degree of certainty can be had only when the mother is appropriated to a particular man as his wife, or to men of one blood as wife, and when women thus appropriated are usually found faithful to their lords.

Considering that the history of all the races of men, so far as we know it, is the history of a progress from the savage state; considering the social condition of rude tribes still upon the earth,—remembering that the races which can be traced in history had all a previous history, which remains unwritten,—it cannot seem a very strange proposition that there has been a stage in the development of human races when there was no

2. It has been doubted whether the blood-tie through the father is entitled to rank with that through the mother. It may be that the connection between father and child is less intimate than that between mother and child as regards the transmission of characteristics, mental or physical. And the former tie is unquestionably less obvious than the latter. It is, however, an undoubted blood-tie, and must have been thought of soon after that through mothers. All that it concerns us to show in the text is, that when the idea of it was formed it could only receive development into a system of kinship on certain conditions, which were not easily satisfied.

3. It will be seen that there may be certainty as to the father's blood (as where all the possible fathers are brothers) without their being certainty as to the father.

such appropriation of women to particular men—when, in short, marriage, as it exists among civilized nations, was not practised. We believe we shall show, to a sufficient degree of probability, that there have been times when marriage, in this sense, was yet undreamt of. Wherever this has been the case the paternity of children must have been uncertain; the conditions essential to a system of kinship through males being formed would therefore be wanting; no such system would be formed; there would be—there could be—kinship through females only.

Not to assume that the progress of the various races of men from savagery has been a uniform process, that all the stages which any of them has gone through have been passed in their order by all, we shall be justified in believing that more or less of promiscuity in the connection of the sexes, and a system of kinship through females only have subsisted among races of men among which no traces of them remain, when we have shown their existence in a considerable number of cases—if in these there appear nothing exceptional. After what has been said above, it must be plain that kinship through females only, if it exists at all, must be a more archaic system of relationship than kinship through males—the product of an earlier and ruder stage in human development than the latter—somewhat more than a step farther back in the direction of savagery. To prove its existence on such a scale as to entitle it to rank among the normal phenomena of human development, is, we may now say, to prove it the most ancient system of kinship. As customs tend to perpetuate themselves and die hard, it will not in any degree make against our explanation of the origin of kinship through females only, that it should be found in some cases along with marriage relations which allow of certainty as to fathers. It is inconceivable that anything but the want of certainty on that point could have long prevented the acknowledgment of kinship through males; and in such cases we shall be able to conclude that such certainty has formerly been wanting—that more or less promiscuous intercourse between the sexes has formerly prevailed. The connection between these two things—uncertain paternity and kinship through females only, seems so necessary—that of cause and effect—that we may confidently infer the one where we find the other.

Let us see, then, what can be said for the proposition that there has been a stage in the progress of men in which a woman was not usually appropriated to a particular man as his wife.

All the evidence we have goes to show that men were from the beginning gregarious. The geological record distinctly exhibits them in groups—naked hunters or feeders upon shell fish leading a precarious life of squalid misery. This testimony is confirmed by all history. We hear nothing in the most ancient times of individuals except as being members of groups. The history of property is the history of the development of proprietary rights *inside* groups, which were at first the only owners,[4] and of all other personal rights—even including the right in offspring—it may be said that their history is that of the gradual assertion of the claims of individuals against the traditional rights of groups.

We, of course, know nothing about the co-ordination of the sexes in the earliest groups. The reader knows already what must be our conjecture as to what it was. We can trace the line of human progress far back towards brutishness; finding as we go back the noble faculties peculiar to man weaker and weaker in their manifestations, producing less and less effect,—at last scarcely any effect at all—upon his position and habits. As we go back, we find more and more in men the traits of gregarious animals; slighter and slighter indications of operative intellect. As among other gregarious animals, the unions of the sexes were probably in the earliest times, loose, transitory, and in some degree promiscuous.

Before the invention of the arts, and the formation of provident habits, the struggle for existence must often have become very serious. The instincts of self-preservation, therefore, must have frequently predominated and shaped the features of society freely, as if the unselfish affections had no place in human nature. None of the races of mankind can have been spared the cruel experience of this initiatory stage; or can have escaped

4. "Ancient Law," *ut supra*, p. 268.

the effects of that experience on its character and customs. Even those most favourably situated must have had long periods of trial, and have suffered from the incessant hostility of neighbours. So, without supposing the course of human events to have been uniform, we must conceive of early human society as having been throughout affected by influences of the same general, unfriendly, character, and as having been determined, though perhaps by unequal pressures, towards one uniform type in all its parts.

Foremost among the results of this early struggle for food and security, must have been an effect upon the balance of the sexes. As braves and hunters were required and valued, it would be the interest of every horde to rear, when possible, its healthy male children. It would be less its interest to rear females, as they would be less capable of self-support, and of contributing, by their exertions, to the common good. In this lies the only explanation which can be accepted of the origin of those systems of female infanticide still existing, the discovery of which from time to time, in out of the way places, so shocks our humanity. It is of no consequence by what theories the races who practise infanticide now defend the practice.[5] There can be no doubt that its origin is everywhere referable to that early time of struggle and necessity which we have been contemplating.

What is now true in varying degrees of all the rudest races may be assumed to have been true of all the earliest groups. We may predicate of the primitive groups that they were all or nearly all marked by a want of balance between the sexes—the males being in the majority. The reader will have little difficulty in granting that we may do so when he reflects on the prevalence of exogamy, the origin of which must be referred to that want of balance. And we think he will be still more ready to make the concession when we shall have surveyed the facts connected with polyandry—the origin of which must be referred to the same cause.

5. Often, as among the Khonds, it is found to be an institution of religion.

What diminished the number of the female sex would increase the importance of women. The first result of the balance of the sexes being against the females, must have been to give every woman more than one, it might be several wooers. Apart from any disproportion of the sexes, we might expect the more engaging females of a horde to be surrounded by suitors. Savages are unrestrained by any sense of delicacy from a copartnery in sexual enjoyments; and, indeed, in the civilised state, the sin of great cities shows that there are no natural restraints sufficient to hold men back from grosser copartneries. But within a horde possessing few women, such copartneries would be a necessity. And as savages assert for themselves a high degree of independence, it is obvious that grave difficulties must have surrounded the constitution and regulation of such copartneries. And to the consideration of these difficulties we are led, the instant we conceive of the primitive groups as containing fewer women than men.

The men of a group must either have quarrelled about their women and separated, splitting the horde into hostile sections; or, in the spirit of indifference, indulged in savage promiscuity. That quarrels and divisions were of frequent occurrence cannot be doubted. These were the first wars for women, and they went to form the habits which established exogamy. And whether quarrels arose or not, we are led to contemplate groups —the horde or its sections—indulging in a promiscuity more or less general. The quarrels must have been between sections of the hordes rather than between individuals. No individual at that stage could well carry off a woman, isolate himself, and found a family. However brave and strong, he could scarcely maintain his independence for any time against numerous assailants. Unless these quarrels went the length of completely disintegrating the groups—a result which the gregarious nature of men tended to prevent—we must arrive at last at groups within which harmony was maintained through indifference and promiscuity.

These groups would hold their women, like their other goods, in common. And the children, while attached to mothers, would belong to the horde.[6] We find traces of the former existence of groups of this description; and it is probable that before the rise of kinship, all the human groups were of that model. On the rise of kinship, the difficulty due to the scarcity of women would more easily be overcome. The first advance from a general promiscuity—assuming its existence—would naturally be to a promiscuity less general—to arrangements between small sets of men to attach themselves to a particular woman. Previous to the establishment of a system of kinship—when men were bound to each other only by the tribal tie—it is obvious that there would constantly be difficulties in the way of their forming such combinations. When, however, the system of kinship through females only, had been firmly established, every group stood resolved into a number of small brotherhoods, each composed of sons of the same mother. And within these, the feeling of close kinship would simplify the constitution of the polyandrous arrangement.

Now, here, at length, we are upon the firm ground of fact. We have examples of general promiscuity; and examples of modified promiscuity, in which, with a pretence of marriage, the woman may bestow her favours upon any one, under certain restrictions as to rank and family. We have numerous examples of polyandry, and they are such as to show that polyandry must be regarded as a modification of and advance from promiscuity. We have examples of polyandry in which the wife has several husbands, who are not necessarily relatives; and very many examples of polyandry in which the husbands are all brothers. We often find these two forms of polyandry in the same district, in different sections of the population: here, the husbands as a rule, are no relations; there, the husbands as a rule, are brothers. Farther, where the husbands are not brothers, we find the system of relationship through females only; and, so enduring is custom, we very often find that system where marriage has long been so regulated as to permit of kin-

6. The tie between mother and child, which exists as a matter of necessity during infancy, is not unfrequently found to be lost sight of among savages on the age of independence being reached. The liability of mothers to be carried off would, among exogamous races, simplify the general filiation of children to the group, rather than to mothers.

ship through males. In many cases we find traces of the system of kinship through females only, lingering about the laws of marriage and succession to estates and titles, even where male kinship has been long established. Moreover, in nearly all the cases in which traces are to be found of kinship through females only, traces of polyandry also remain. Thus, what we find is just what was to be expected if the account we have offered of the origin of polyandry were correct.

We repeat, that in showing the prevalence of polyandry, we shall be showing the prevalence of a modification of promiscuity. This is manifest as regards the ruder species of polyandry, in which the husbands are not relations. It is equally, though less obviously, true of the less rude polyandry in which the husbands are brothers. From the way in which polyandry is presented to us, we shall have a proof that the less rude polyandry was developed from the ruder by the help of the system of kinship through females only—was superinduced, that is, upon a promiscuity less qualified than itself. Promiscuity, producing uncertainty of fatherhood, led to the system of kinship through mothers only. This kinship paved the way for polyandry such as we commonly find it; and this form of polyandry introduced male kinship.[7] That, along with the ruder polyandry, we always find the system of kinship through females only, and that where the less rude form prevails we can generally trace that system, is moreover a proof *a posteriori* of what we have shown must be the case, that the origin of kinship through females only is referable to uncertainty of male parentage.

We shall not concern ourselves with the direct evidence which might be adduced to show that there once prevailed among men a promiscuity less qualified than polyandry. We may however recall the fact, that tradition is found everywhere pointing to a time when marriage was unknown, and to some

7. We shall see farther on how numerous the known cases are in which the progress to male kinship and the patriarchal system was a progress having this kind of polyandry for one of its stages. The other main highway of progress must have lain through the system of confining women —a system probably established by exogamy and the practice of capturing wives.

legislator to whom it owed its institution: among the Egyptians to Menes; the Chinese to Fohi; the Greeks to Cecrops; the Hindus to Svetaketu.[8] And we shall proceed to show how much evidence remains to give verisimilitude to these traditions. Passing over communities in which, according to ancient historians, something like a general promiscuity prevailed—such as the Massagetae, Agathyrsi, and the ancient Spartans; passing over also the numerous races now existing, which, according to modern travellers, have no conception of conjugal fidelity[9]—we

8. See Muir's Sanskrit Texts, 1860. Part ii. p. 336.

9. It may be as well to append some modern examples of promiscuity, and of practices which have the same effect in rendering uncertain male parentage. The Ansarians have their wives in common; the people of Martawan, of the tribe of Ansarians, let out their wives and daughters (Volney, "Travels," chap. xxvii.) The Keiaz (Paropamisans) lend their wives to their guests (Latham, "Des. Ethn.," vol. ii. p. 246); so do the Eimauk (Caubul),—Elphinstone, 1815, p. 483; so, we are informed, do the Kandyans. The Mpongme (Africa) lend wives (Reade, "Sav. Afr.," p. 259); so do the Koryaks and Chukchi, who lend out daughters as well (N. E. Siberia)—Erman, vol. ii. p. 531, and v. Cochrane's "Journey," 1825, vol. i. p. 336. The Koryaks are also polyandrous. The same disregard of conjugal fidelity appeared in Caindu, Cascar (Turkistan Tartary), and in Cumana (Gaya, p. 104; Marco Polo, ut infra, p. 258). We find it now among the Aimaks ("Des. Ethn.," vol. i. p. 333). It was customary in Kamul (Marco Polo, Bohn's edition, p. 110). Montesquieu, b. 16, c. viii., remarks on the licentious wantonness of the women of Patan, against which the men had to adopt measures of self-protection. Mr. Wilson of Mussoorie, in an admirable report on the Puharies of Gurwhal ("A Summer Ramble in the Himalayas," q. v. p. 182), says of the Gungarees and Perbuttees: "Their immorality is something incredible—chastity being little appreciated, even where it does exist." In various other quarters we find practices fatal to certainty of male parentage, such as frequent divorces, e. g., among the Bedouins, Burckhardt, "Notes," I. 111; and marriages for an agreed upon term of endurance, usually short. Such marriages were usual in Sounan, Arabia Felix (Hamilton's "New Account of the East Indies," vol. i. p. 51); in Siam (Id., vol. ii. p. 279). In China such marriages are said to be still customary. In a recent report of the proceedings of the Society of Sainte-Enfance in China, in the Esperance of Nancy, it is said that, in many parts, Chinamen may repudiate their wives, and marry again, every year. As a result, the children belong to the mother, who has over them the power of life or death. The same must have been the case in Turkistan (Marco Polo, ut supra, p. 99). According to Livingstone ("Travels," p. 394), marriage in Loando is almost unknown—an unsettled concubinage. And see Idem, p. 436, for an example of savage indifference as to marital purity. In the Polynesian Mythology, we have an excellent casual proof

shall now go on to consider the regulated promiscuity known as polyandry, and see to what extent it exists, and what traces of its former existence still remain.

Let us first see what is the area over which polyandry now prevails. It prevails universally in Tibet, and is common in the Himalayan and Sub-Himalayan regions adjoining Tibet; in the valley of Kashmir; among the Spiti, in Ladak; in Kistewar and Sirmor. It occurs among the Telingese; in the Sivalik mountains, and in Kasia. There are unmistakeable traces of its existence till recently in Gurwhal, Sylhet and Cachar. Farther south in India we find polyandry among the Tudas of the Nilgherry Hills, the Coorgs of Mysore, and the Nairs, the Maleres, and Poleres of Malabar. We find it off the Indian coast in Ceylon; and going eastward strike on it as an ancient though now almost superseded custom in New Zealand, and in one or two of the Pacific Islands. Going northward we meet it again in the Aleutian Islands; and taking the continent to the west and north of the Aleutians we find it among the Koryaks to the north of the Okhotsk Sea. Crossing the Russian Empire to the west side we find polyandry among the Saporogian Cossacks; we thus have traced it at points half round the globe. This is not all, however. Polyandry is found in several parts of Africa and of America. We have the authority of Humboldt for its prevalence among the tribes on the Orinocco, and he also vouches for its former prevalence in Lancerota one of the Canary Islands.[10]

---

of the uncertainty of male parentage, even where there is marriage (polygamous). A young man distinguishes himself, and turns out to be the chief's son. He was "a young man, the name of whose father had never been told by his mother." The lady was one of the chief's wives! And see Turner's "Tibet," p. 10, and McCulloch's "Munnipore," for examples of a system of pawning wives. See also, for similar or worse customs, Buchanan's "Journey from Madras," 1807, vol. ii. pp. 129, 492, and vol. iii. p. 66; Krusenstern's "Voyage," 1813, vol. ii. p. 245 (Kamschatka); La Perouse's "Voyage," 1798, vol. ii. p. 195 (Island of Maouna); Mandeville, chap. xxiii. (Chatay); and Huc's "Travels," vol. ii. p. 142, Nat. Illus. Lib.

10. Turner's "Tibet," 1800, p. 348. Vigne's "Kashmir," 1842, vol. i. p. 37. Cunningham's "Ladak," 1854, p. 306. Buchanan's "Journey," etc., 1807, vol. ii. pp. 408–12. Archer's "Upper India," 1833, vol. i. p. 185. Latham's "Descriptive Ethnology," 1859, vol. i. pp. 24–28; vol. ii. pp. 398, 496, and 462. Humboldt's "Personal Narrative" (William's Transla-

From ancient history we learn that polyandry at one time existed over even a greater area. Traces of it remained in the time of Tacitus among the Germans.[11] And while in certain cantons of Media, according to Strabo,[12] polygynia was authorised by express law which ordained every inhabitant to maintain at least seven wives; in other cantons the opposite rule was in force: a woman was allowed to have many husbands, and they looked with contempt on those who had less than five. Caesar informs us that in his time polyandry prevailed among the Britons.[13] We find direct evidence of its existence among the Picts in the Irish Nennius,[14] not to mention traces of it in the Pictish Laws of Succession. Further we find traditions of it among the Hindus[15]—especially among the Rajputs. And we find it among the Getes of Transaxiana (the Yuti or Yuechi of the Chinese historians).[16] To see where else it prevailed we must go back upon our authorities and examine the various phases of polyandry which they present, and obtain a test for detecting its presence where historical evidence of its existence is awanting.

The ruder form of polyandry, as we have said, is that in which the husbands are *not* brothers; the less rude is that in which they *are* brothers. The polyandry of the Kasias, the Nairs, and the Saporogian Cossacks, appears to be purely of the ruder sort, and is attended by the system of kinship through females

---

tion), 1819, chap. i., vol. i. p. 84, and vol. v., part ii., p. 549. Hamilton's "New Account of the East Indies," 1727, vol. i. pp. 274 and 308. Reade's "Savage Africa," p. 43. Erman's "Travels in Siberia," vol. ii. p. 531. "Marriage Ceremonies," by Seignior Gaya, 1698, pp. 70 and 96. Tennent's "Ceylon," 1859, vol. ii. p. 429. "Legend of Rupe," Grey's "Polynesian Mythology," 1854, p. 81. "A Summer Ramble in the Himalayas," 1860, p. 202. Fisher's "Memoir of Sylhet, etc.," in Journal of Asiatic Soc., Bengal, vol. ix. p. 834. "Asiat. Res.," vol. v. p. 13. Our information regarding the Saporogian Cossacks has been obtained from Sir John M'Neil.

11. "German." xx., Latham's Edn., p. 67, *et seq.*

12. Lib. ii. p. 798; and see Goguet, vol. iii. book vi. c. i.

13. "De Bello Gallico," lib. v., c. xiv.

14. Appendix LI.

15. Tod's "Annals, etc., of Rajasthan," 1829, p. 48; and see Max Müller's "Hist. of Sans. Anc. Lit." pp. 45, *et seq.*; Tod's "Travels," 1839, p. 464.

16. Tod's "Travels," *ut supra.*

only. It is left doubtful what is the form of the institution in some instances, as in the Aleutian Islands, and among the Koryaks. But in all the other cases in which polyandry occurs, the authorities show that the ruder form occurs among the lower classes wherever the less rude occurs, except in Tibet, where polyandry is universal and the husbands are always brothers; except in Malabar, where polyandry is universally practised by all classes, saving the Brahmans only, but is of the ruder species among the high caste Nairs, and of the less rude among the lower castes, the Teers, Maleres, and Poleres. It is in the nature of the case that all the possible forms of polyandry must lie in between, or be embraced in, the Nair and Tibetan forms.

Let us attend then to the accounts we have of these two forms. Of the Nair polyandry we have three accounts. The account in the "Asiatic Researches" [17] is that among the Nairs it is the custom for one woman "to have attached to her two males, or four, or perhaps more, and they cohabit according to rules." With this account that of Hamilton agrees,[18] excepting that he states that a Nair woman could have no more than twelve husbands, and had to select these under certain restrictions as to rank and caste. On the other hand, Buchanan states[19] that the women after marriage[20] are free to cohabit with any number of men, under certain restrictions as to tribe and caste. It is consistent with the three accounts, and is directly stated by Hamilton, that a Nair may be one in several combinations of husbands; that is, he may have any number of wives. The accounts, however, differ in regard to one important particular. Buchanan represents the wife as living in family with her mother or brother, while Hamilton represents her as having "an house built for her own conveniency" on being married to the first of her husbands. In the "Asiatic Researches" the wife is represented as living with her mother or brother.

17. Vol. v. p. 13
18. "Account of the East Indies," *ut supra*, vol. i. p. 308.
19. Buchanan's "Journey," vol. ii. p. 411.
20. In the "Asiatic Researches" it is said, "The Nairs practice not marriage, except as far as may be implied from their tying a thread round the neck of the woman on the first occasion."

The probability is that both arrangements are occasionally adopted, the more usual course being for the wife to remain in the family of her mother and brothers. In Ceylon, where the higher and lower polyandry co-exist, marriage is of two sorts— Deega or Beena—according as the wife goes to live in the house and village of her husbands, or as the husband or husbands come to live with her in or near the house of her birth.[21] And among the Kandyans the rights of inheritance of a woman and her children are found to depend on whether the woman is a beena or a deega wife.

The three accounts which we have of the Nair polyandry are agreed that the Nair husbands are usually not brothers—usually not relatives—and that the institution leaves male parentage and the father's blood quite uncertain. "In consequence of this strange manner of propagating the species," says Buchanan,[22]

> no Nair knows his father, and every man looks upon his sister's children as his heirs. He indeed looks upon them with the same fondness that fathers in other parts of the world have for their own children, and he would be considered as an unnatural monster were he to show such signs of grief at the death of a child, which from long cohabitation and love with its mother, he might suppose to be his own, as he did at the death of a child of his sister. A man's mother manages his family; and after her death his eldest sister assumes the direction. *Brothers almost always live under the same roof;* but if one of the family separates from the rest he is always accompanied by his favourite sister. A man's movable property, after his death, is divided among the sons and daughters of all his sisters; and if there are lands, their management falls *to the eldest male of the family.*[23]

21. See Forbes' "Ceylon," 1840, vol. i. p. 333. Mr. Starke, late Chief-Justice of Ceylon, says that "sometimes a deega married girl returned to her parents' house and was there provided with a beena husband who lived with her in family" (private letter). The beena husband's tenure of office seems to have been very insecure. See Forbes, *ut supra.* The Kandyans are now under British rule, and their marriages regulated by a special ordinance.

22. *Ut supra*, vol. ii. p. 412.

23. See Buchanan, vol. ii. p. 594.

Now here, derived from the ruder polyandry, is an exceedingly rude, *the rudest,* form of family system with which we are acquainted. And it is a sort of family system which is found, more or less modified in some of its features, in several cases, where marriage is now either monogamous or polygamous. Its chief features are the absence of a paternal head, and the system of female succession. Among the Kocch, with whom marriage is now monogamous, we find the same system, excepting that the family circle includes the daughter's husband, as a subordinate member of the family. A Kocch man goes, on his marriage, like the beena husband of Ceylon, to live in family with his wife and her mother; on his marriage all his property is made over to his wife; and on her death her heirs are her daughters.[24] Here we conclude that the advance from the ruder polyandry to monogamy took place in some way consistent with the preservation of the main features of the family system peculiar to the ruder polyandry—consistent with the mother's maintaining her position as the head of the family, and with an increase of the influence of women as connecting links in the social and proprietary systems. We shall presently see that the advance in this direction must be counted exceptional; at the same time it cannot well be doubted that such a family system as we find among the Kocch had its origin in the ruder species of polyandry.

What, then, was the normal line of progress? We think that we shall be able to show what it was—that it lay between the lower and higher polyandry. In the accounts we have, we can detect stages of preparation for the change from the former species of polyandry to the latter. We must regard as the rudest cases those in which the wife lives not with her husbands, but with her mother or brothers. In these cases a woman's children are born in and belong to *her* mother's house. In the cases next in order of rudeness, the wife passes into cohabitation, according to fixed rules, with the husbands, in a house of her own—becoming thus detached from her family, though still connected with it through the right of her children to become heirs to the family estate. Her children would still belong to

24. "Des. Ethn.," vol. i. p. 96.

her mother's family—the want of a community of blood and interests among the husbands preventing the appropriation of the children to them. Such cases, however—detaching the woman from her family—would prepare the way for a species of marriage still less rude, in which the woman passed from her family, not into a house of her own, but into the family of her husbands, in which her children would be born, and to which they would belong. This could only happen when the husbands were all of one blood, and had common rights of property—in short, when they were brothers.

This last was a most important step in advance. The girl of a house no longer remained at home with her mother and brothers—aiding in and succeeding to the management; she passed into another family, associating with the sons thereof as wife; while her place at home was assumed by a stranger—as wife to her brothers. There being now a community of blood and interests in the husbands, there was nothing to prevent the appropriation to them of her children—an appropriation which would disqualify the children for being heirs to the property of her mother and brothers. To give effect now to the old law of succession, would be, not to keep property in families, but to introduce a system of exchanges of family estates. Moreover, when this form of marriage became general, and when conjugal fidelity was secured by penalties, we should expect to find that the system of kinship through males would appear—this species of marriage allowing of certainty as to the father's blood, though not of certainty as to fathers. A woman's children would become the heirs of the husband's family in which they would be born, and to which they would belong.

Now it is this highest development of polyandry, and of the family system which polyandry admitted of, which we find in Tibet.

"Here," says Turner, speaking of Tibet,[25]

> we find a practice—that of polyandry—universally prevailing; and see one female associating her fate and fortune with all the brothers of a family, without any

25. Turner's "Tibet," 1800, p. 348.

restriction of age or of numbers. The choice of a wife is the privilege of the elder brother. . . . The number of husbands is not, as far as I could learn, defined or restricted within any limits; it sometimes happens that in a small family there is but one male; and the number, perhaps, may seldom exceed that which a native of rank, during my residence at Teshoo Loomboo, pointed out to me in a family resident in the neighbourhood, in which five brothers were then living very happily with one female, under the same connubial compact. Nor is this sort of league confined to the lower ranks of people alone: it is found also frequently in the most opulent families.

Let us now see to what extent polyandry of the Tibetan type can be traced elsewhere than in Tibet; and what evidence there is of its being an advance from the Nair species of polyandry. The authorities already cited [26] exhibit the Tibetan as the prevailing species of polyandry in nearly the whole of the Himalayan and sub-Himalayan regions: Kashmir, Ladak, Kinawer, Kistewar, and Sirmor. It is the general form of polyandry in Ceylon. It is the form which Humboldt found among the red-men. "Among the Avaroes and the Maypures," he says, "brothers have often but one wife." It is the form which Caesar found among the Britons. "Uxores habent deni duodenique inter se communes, *et maxime* fratres cum fratribus, et parentes cum liberis; sed si qui sunt ex his nati, eorum habentur liberi a quibus primum virgines quaeque ductae sunt." [27] And to show that the two forms of polyandry are stages in a progress, we repeat that almost everywhere, outside Tibet, we find the lower form accompanying the higher. In some quarters the lower only is known—as in Kasia and among the Nairs. In others—Kooloo, for example—the lower form is prevalent; the higher[28] also is

26. *Ante*, p. 73.
27. "De Bello Gallico," v. xiv.
28. Archer, in his "Upper India" (1833), v. i. pp. 235–36, says of the Grooah (Kooloo): "Here one woman cohabits with two, three, and four men, *and they may even be all brothers;* this practice is universal. I was informed of the rules and modes of intercourse, all evincing a state of society least beholden to civilization, or less sophisticated than any yet known."

known, but is exceptional. Again, in numerous quarters the higher is the general form, and the lower the exceptional—as in Ceylon; and lastly, in some quarters, as in Tibet, we lose sight of the lower form altogether. The higher polyandry has become a national institution.

And finding the higher polyandry a national institution, we observe that we are in a position to show that most probably polyandry formerly prevailed over a still vaster area than that within which we have hitherto found it. We have seen that with polyandry, of the Tibetan type, wherever it was long and generally established, kinship through males must have been introduced; the father's blood, though not the father, being certain, where the wife was faithful. We have also seen, in the case of the Britons, that the children of the woman were accounted to belong to the husband who first espoused her; and that in Tibet, the right of choosing the wife belongs to the eldest brother, to whom, also, the children of the marriage are held to belong. We must now, to obtain what we have been in search of—a test of the former presence of polyandry—look at the Tibetan form of polyandry in a state of decadence. We find it in such a state in Ladak. "In Ladak," says Moorcroft,[29]

> when an eldest son marries, the property of his father (more properly the family estate) descends to him, and he is charged with the maintenance of his parents. The parents may continue to live with him, if he and his wife please; if not, a separate dwelling is provided for them.[30] A younger son is usually made a Lama. Should there be more brothers, *and they agree to the arrangement*, the juniors become inferior husbands to the wife; all the children, however, are considered as belonging to the head of the family. The younger brothers have no authority; they wait upon the elder as his servants, and can be turned out of doors at his pleasure, without it being incumbent upon him to provide for them. *On the death of the eldest brother, his property, authority, and widow, devolve upon his next brother.*

29. Moorcroft's and Trebeck's "Travels," 1841, v. i. p. 320.
30. See McCulloch's "Munnipore," pp. 8 and 67, for a similar custom among the Loohoopas.

And that whether the younger brother has agreed to the poly-androus arrangement or not. He has a customary right of succession to his brother's property, and to his widow, and he cannot take the one without taking the other.

Here we are brought to consider the meaning and origin of the legal obligation which we find laid on younger brothers, among certain peoples, to marry in their turn the widow of their deceased elder brother. There can be no doubt that that obligation was in its origin the counterpart of a legal right of succession. It is so with the Kirghiz, Aenezes, and Mongols—the next brother being heir even where the elder leaves is-sue.

When history begins, the Hebrew law preferred the issue to the next brother; but when he or the next of kin succeeded, it was on the old footing. This is clear from the book of Ruth.[31] The *hereditatis emptor* of the deceased took to wife at the same time his widow, "to raise up the name of the dead upon his inheritance." The obligation to marry the widow was the counterpart of the right of succession. And we can see the connection between the obligation and heirship dropping slowly out of view. In Deuteronomy[32] it is provided that the husband's brother shall "perform the duty of an husband's brother" to the widow, only when the brethren dwell together, and one of them dies childless. The obligation is here presented pure—as *a duty* falling on the brother, which it was disgraceful to neglect.

In India, by the time when the Institutes of Menu were com-piled, the obligation was laid on the brother only in case the deceased left no son. Grave doubts had arisen as to the extent and propriety of the obligation, the number of sons to be be-gotten on the widow,[33] and the terms on which the brother should live with her. "The first object of the appointment being obtained, according to law, both the brother and the widow must live together like a father and daughter by affinity." Again, it is doubted whether the obligation extends to the twice-born

31. Chap. iv. ver. 6.
32. Chap. xxv. ver. 5–10.
33. Chap. ix. ver. 61, 62.

classes. "Such a commission to a brother or other near kinsman is nowhere mentioned in the nuptial texts of the Veda. . . . This practice, fit only for cattle, is reprehended by learned Brahmans; yet it is declared to have been the practice even of men while Vena had sovereign power." [34] Yet elsewhere in the code the obligation is contemplated as legal, and provision is made for the rights of succession of the issue of the Levirate union. "Should a younger brother have begotten a son on the wife of his deceased elder brother, the division (of the estate) must then be made equally between that son, who represents the deceased, and his natural father: thus is the law settled." We repeat, that in Menu's time the obligation had not only been, to some extent, dissociated from the corresponding right of inheritance, but was falling into disrepute. We see it also falling into desuetude among the Hebrews. In the earliest age the Levir had no alternative but to take the widow; *indeed she was his wife without any form of marriage.*[35] By the Mosaic Law, however, he might get quit of her if he chose by submitting to the ceremony of "loosing the shoe."

It is impossible not to believe that we have here presented to us successive stages of decay of one and the same original institution; impossible not to connect the obligation, in its several phases, with what we have seen prevailing in Ladak; impossible not to regard it as having originally been a right of succession, or the counterpart of such a right, derived from the practice of polyandry. Regarded as in its origin a right of succession, it exhibits the next younger brother as succeeding to the universitas of the elder—taking up all his rights and obligations—*inter alia,* his widow. But how came the right of succession to open, as in the ruder cases, to the brother in preference to the son of the deceased? We repeat, that the only explanation that can be given of this is, that the law of succession was derived from polyandry. The succession of brothers to one another, in order of age, is a feature of the law of succession under both forms of polyandry. Under the ruder, brothers succeed one another; and failing brothers, the sister's children come in:

34. Chap. ix. ver. 66.
35. Lewis' "Hebrew Republic," 1725, vol. iii. p. 268.

under the less rude, brothers succeed one another; and failing brothers, comes in the eldest son of the brotherhood. And nowhere, excepting where there is or has been polyandry, have we such a system of succession—brothers succeeding in preference to sons.

The same conclusion is forced upon us from another point of view. In the lowest cases of polyandry the children belong to the mother; in the more advanced to the eldest brother (an approach towards agnation). Now the peculiarity of the obligation is, in all cases, that it was an obligation "to raise up seed" to the older brother. The children begotten by the younger brother were accounted the children of the elder deceased. It is obvious that it could more easily be feigned that the children belonged to the brother deceased, if already, at a prior stage, the children of the brotherhood had been accounted the children of the eldest brother, i.e., if we suppose the obligation to be a relic of polyandry.

Curiously enough, Dr. Latham would invert the order of development by producing the ruder fact—polyandry—from the less rude obligation. But, clearly, this is an inversion of the order of nature—which is progressive—in which the ruder gives birth to the less rude, not the less rude to the ruder.[36]

Assuming the correctness of this view of the origin of that obligation, we must hold that polyandry in the Tibetan form prevailed at one time throughout India.[37] Among the race from which the ancient Hebrews were descended; among the Moabites and the ancient Persians.[38] Among the Druses and all the Arab tribes in Syria;[39] the Mongols, Ostiaks, Kirghiz Turks, and tribes of the Caucasus.[40] Among the Makololo, and, we

36. The subject of polyandry has been most carelessly, it seems to us, handled by Dr. Latham. It is enough to refer to "Des. Ethn.," vol. ii. p. 463, et seq., where he recklessly lays it down that the descensus per umbilicum is part and parcel of polyandry.
37. "Institute of Menu," c. iii., § 173, and c. ix., § 57–58, and § 182; "Asi. Res.," vol. iii. p. 28.
38. Deut. xxv. 5–11; Ruth i. 11–13; Kleuker "Zendavesta," iii. p. 226.
39. Volney's "Travels," vol. ii. p. 807; Burckhardt's "Notes," vol. i. 112.
40. "Des. Ethn.," vol. i. pp. 312, 346, and 455; Haxthausen, "Trans-Caucasia," p. 403.

may believe, many other peoples in Africa.[41] It is needless to repeat that we must also conclude that among the peoples just enumerated the Tibetan form of polyandry was preceded by the Nair, and, at a still earlier date, by utter promiscuity.

We have found polyandry in so many lands, among so many races, and in such phases of progressive development, that we are surely justified in classing it among the phenomena most distinctive of—the most likely to occur at—the earlier stages of the progress of any race of men. Its origin can only be ascribed to a scarcity of women as compared to men. And the vast area over which it anciently prevailed, can leave no doubt in the mind that in former times the balance of the sexes must have been seriously disturbed (artificially), and that we were right in predicating of the primitive groups that they usually contained fewer women than men. When the phenomena of exogamy—also due to a scarcity of women—are contemplated along with the phenomena of polyandry, the impression of this fact produced on the mind is almost as strong as the feeling produced by demonstration. To whatever extent a want of balance between the sexes prevailed, to that extent certainty as to male parentage was in the earlier stages of progress excluded. With polyandry itself there is uncertainty upon this point. In the lower cases the uncertainty is absolute. And regarding, as we must do, the higher as an advance from the lower, we are forced to conclude that wherever we have found polyandry, or traces of it, there must anciently have prevailed the system of kinship through females only.

In a preceding chapter we found the system of kinship through females only, universally prevailing among the Australian Blacks;[42] prevailing among the majority of the nations of the American Red-men;[43] and among the South Sea Islanders.[44] That is, we found it among peoples now practising polygunia, and which have advanced far towards the patriarchal system. We infer that with these peoples the unions of the

41. Livingstone, p. 185.
42. Ante, p. 47.
43. Ante, p. 51.
44. Ante, p. 52.

sexes were originally promiscuous or polyandrous. With regard to the Red-men, indeed, there is little room for doubting that they formerly all practised polyandry. It is now occasionally to be found among them, and their system of relationship—their names for kinsmen and kinswomen—point to its having been their universal custom. Mr. Morgan of Rochester, New York, whose account of the Indian nations we have already had occasion to refer to, gives the following as radical features of the system of relationship prevailing among them: 1. "All the brothers of a father are equally fathers to his children (this where there is now no polyandry). 2. All the children of several brothers are brothers and sisters to each other; all the grandsons of a man's brothers are his grandsons." [45] These features of the system bear the stamp of a polyandrous origin; [46] they are features of the system of relationship which might be expected to accompany the higher polyandry. The schedules returned to Mr. Morgan show that among the Tamul and Telugu, peoples of Southern India, numbering about twenty-four millions, "all the brothers of a father are usually called fathers, but in strictness, those who are older than the father are called *great fathers*, and those who are younger, *little fathers*." And both the Tamul and Telugu are still, as we have seen, to some extent polyandrous. The same system of relationship is found among the Puharies, a people on the skirts of the Tibetan region, and that manifestly practised polyandry till a late date. With the Puharies, all the brothers of a father are equally fathers to his children. [47]

45. Camb. Journ., 1860, pp. 144, 145.
46. It may be asked why the Red-men should not now have kinship through males if they have passed, as they appear to have done, through the stage of polyandry of the Tibetan type. Our answer is, that in some cases *they have* male kinships, and that probably in Australia, and among the majority of the nations of the Red-men, the earlier species of kinship has been perpetuated by the system of capturing wives. We shall hereafter see that the system of capture introduces uncertainty as to male parentage, independently of the causes of such uncertainty which we have been considering. We shall also see that all polyandrous peoples may not have been exogamous, while all exogamous peoples *must* have been polyandrous.
47. Report of Mr. Wilson, *ut supra.*

We have seen that the Kasias, the Nairs, and the Saporogian Cossacks, have the system of kinship through females only. We find that system in Tulava, in the neighbourhood of the Nairs. "Among the Buntar"—the highest rank of Sudras in Tulava—"a man's children," says Buchanan, "are not his heirs. During his lifetime he may give them money; but all of which he dies possessed goes to his sisters and to their children." The cause must be the same in either case, though marriage in Tulava has shifted from polyandry to polygunia.[48] Among the Rajputs we have traces of the system of female kinship.[49] The Kocch have kinship and succession through females only; and so have the *But* (Bodo).[50] Farther, we find that system among the Banyai,[51] in Ashanti, Aquapim, and Congo, and are assured that traces of it are to be found all over Africa.[52] We have already had occasion to notice its occurrence among the Chinese.[53]

Let us now see what evidence there is of the former existence of the system of kinship through females only. We recall the fact that, in an earlier chapter, we saw reason to believe that it anciently prevailed among the Celts.[54] We infer that among the Celts there was anciently no certainty of male parentage. We now notice that we find traces of such a system in India in the Sutras of Gautama. In these, marriage with the daughter of a maternal uncle—a cousin on the mother's side—is emphatically prohibited as being clearly against the principles of the sacred writings.[55] Such a prohibition, found with an exogamous race—and almost all the Indian races were and are, as we have seen, exogamous—can be referred only to the system of kinship through females only. And it is impossible to avoid connecting with this the tradition that the five Pandava princes—brothers so called—were husbands of one wife. "How

48. Buchanan, *ut supra*, vol. iii., p. 16.
49. Tod's "Annals," etc., *ut supra*, p. 48.
50. "Des. Ethn.," vol. i., pp. 96, 109.
51. Livingstone's "Travels," pp. 617–22.
52. Reade's "Savage Africa," p. 43.
53. *Ante*, p. 72.
54. *Ante*, pp. 52–53.
55. Max Müller's "Hist. of Anc. Sans. Liter.," 1859, p. 53.

is it," asks Max Müller,[56] in discussing the character of the Mahabharata,

> that the five Pandava princes who are at first represented as receiving so strictly Brahmanic an education, could afterwards have been married to *one* wife? This is in plain opposition to Brahmanic law, where it is said "they are many wives of one man; not many husbands of one wife." Such a contradiction can only be accounted for by the admission that in this case epic tradition in the mouth of the people was too strong to allow this essential and curious feature in the life of its heroes to be changed.

In other words, we have here the tradition "that the races among whom the five principal heroes of the Mahabharata were born and fostered," practised polyandry. This is confirmed by all that is related of the Pandava princes. They were the reputed sons of Pandu,—but, in fact, three of them were sons of one of his wives by three different gods, and the other two were sons of another wife by the Aswini-Kumaras.[57] Pandu himself was the son of a marriage with a brother's widow. When the five princes married one wife, the eldest was first married to her by the family priest, and then the other four in their order, according to priority of birth. The princes are represented as living in family with Kauli, their mother—the head of their house. In the poem, Bishma, their granduncle—

56. *Idem*, p. 46.

57. [Monier-] Williams' "Indian Epic Poetry," 1863, p. 17. It is worthy of notice that in a passage of the Mahabharata, Book i., vv. 4719–22, which has been translated by Dr. Muir ("Sanskrit Texts," Part ii. p. 336), we have the following account of the freedom of women in the early world. "Women were formerly unconfined, and roved about at their pleasure, independent (within their respective castes). Though in their youthful innocence they abandoned their husbands, they were guilty of no offence; for such was the rule in early times. This ancient custom is even now the law for creatures born as brutes, which are free from lust and anger. This custom is supported by authority, and is observed by great Rishis, and *it is still practised among the Northern Kurus*." In a note, Dr. Muir adds that the practice of promiscuous intercourse was, according to the legend, abolished by Svetaketu, son of the Rishi Uddalaka, who was incensed at seeing his mother led away by a strange Brahman. Svetaketu established conjugal fidelity.

grandfather's brother—is often styled *their grandfather;* and though Bishma was really the uncle—father's brother—of Pandu, he is sometimes styled *his father.*[58] All these circumstances point to a system of polyandry of the Tibetan type. The very terminology is that of polyandry, and which polyandry has left behind it among the Tamul, the Telugu, the Puharies, and the Red-men of America. In short, though the original tradition has obviously been tampered with, enough of it remains to oblige us to acknowledge it as a genuine tradition of a stage of Aryan civilization, when the marriage system was polyandrous as it is now in Tibet. It is almost needless to point out that we have, in this tradition, a confirmation of our view of the origin of the obligation which, in the code of Menu, is recognised as imposed on brothers in turn to marry the widow of a brother deceased. We shall find a further confirmation of that view in the case of the Hebrews.

We are not without evidence of the existence in early times of the system of female kinship among the Semitic races. It would appear that while Abraham still lived, his tribesmen as yet recognised only that primitive kinship in some important relations in life—*e.g.,* as affecting the right of intermarriage. Between the times of Abraham and the promulgation of the Levitical law, a complete revolution took place in Jewish custom. The patriarch himself married his sister-german, or by the same father; and his brother Nahor married his niece,[59] the daughter of a brother. So Amram, the father of Moses and Aaron, married his father's sister (Exod. vi. 20). These women were not relatives, in a full legal sense, of their husbands. They were connected with them through males only, and through males in those times there was not, as yet, a perfect kinship. We have similar evidence of the existence of the system of kinship, through females only, among the Phoenicians.[60]

Among the Greeks, traces of this early law remained in historic times. To pass over the tradition that in Greece before

58. See [Monier-] Williams' "Indian Epic Poetry," 1863, pp. 93, 99, and 114.
59. Genesis xi. 26–29; and see xx. 12.
60. "Achilles Tatius," lib. i.

Cecrops children always bore the names of their mothers,[61] we have the fact that at Athens a brother might marry a sister-german, but not a sister-uterine or consanguineous. Here again we have a relic of the doctrine that a child had no paternal relatives. A sister-uterine was a near kinswoman, but a sister-german was no kinswoman at all. Montesquieu[62] ascribes this Athenian rule to a device of the legislature for regulating successions; but he belongs to the class of philosophers who make more of enactments than of popular usages. As Bunsen[63] has pointed out, there can be no doubt that the true meaning and origin of the rule were what we have indicated.

There is one case which might be cited to throw doubt upon some of the conclusions at which we have arrived in this chapter. This is the report of Philo, that the Spartans allowed a man to marry his sister-uterine, but not his sister-german, or by the same father.[64] This may have been circulated for the sake of the contrast which it presented to Athenian custom; at any rate, we hold it to be incredible—as discordant with old law as with the habits of the Lacedaemonians. It is beyond belief that there was this superior regard for the father's blood in ancient Sparta, where the marriage tie was so loose that men lent their wives to one another, and cared little by whom children were begotten, provided they turned out strong and healthy. It is incredible, that in a community where any sort of importance was attached to blood, the unquestionable blood tie between children of the same mother should be so disregarded. If we are to credit the report at all, it must be on the supposition that the Spartans were exceptional in their development like the ancient Persians (from whom the Druses derived their customs). And we do not regard the case of the Persians as of weight against our reasoning, but the contrary. The Per-

61. Varro, apud Aigust.: de Civ. Dei, l. 18, c. 9. Suidas, voce προμηθ, t. 3, p. 189; and v. Goguet, B. i., vol. 2.

62. Book v., c. 5.

63. De Jure Hered. Athen., p. 148; Gottingen, 1813.

64. The reader may suspect that this is a relic of strict agnatic law. But for the reasons stated in the text, we hold that view to be excluded. The system of relationship, through males only, has never, in any well authenticated case, been developed into such a rule as this.

sian customs were just those of hordes who consecrated an incestuous promiscuity into a system. If they allowed the marriages of brothers and sisters consanguineous, they also sanctioned the unions of sons and mothers, and of fathers and daughters, and in some cases required them for the purposes of religion.[65]

At the outset of our argument we saw that if the system of kinship through females only could be shown to exist, or to have existed, it must be accounted a more archaic system of kinship than the system of relationship through males,—the product of an earlier and ruder stage in human development; and that to prove its existence on such a scale as to entitle it to rank among the normal phenomena of human development would be to prove it the most ancient system of kinship. We now submit that we have amply established our proposition. We have collected abundant evidence of the nonexistence in many places of the conditions necessary for the rise of kinship through males; in many of these cases—some of them cases of great populations—we have been able to adduce evidence of the existence of the system of kinship through females only. We have seen that polyandry must be accepted as a stage in the progress towards marriage proper and the patriarchal system. The lower forms of polyandry we have found to be accompanied by the system of kinship through females only. We have seen polyandry change its form till it allowed of kinship through males, and then die away into an obligation on younger brothers in turn to espouse the widow of the eldest brother; and in some cases, Indo-European as well as Semitic, in which we found that relic of polyandry, we have found, or found traces of, the system of kinship through females only. Had the facts bearing on our inquiry ever been systematically observed, noted, and collected, it is probable our case might be made to appear stronger than it does. But as it is, we submit that we have done quite enough to establish the truth of our proposition.

Before leaving this subject we would observe that, whether the system of kinship through females only prevailed uni-

65. See a full account of the Persian customs in Selden's "Jus Naturale," *ut supra*, chap. xi.

versally at the first or not, it must have prevailed wherever exogamy prevailed—exogamy and the consequent practice of capturing wives. Certainty as to fathers is impossible where mothers are stolen from their first lords, and liable to be re-stolen before the birth of children. And as exogamy and poly-andry are referable to one and the same cause—a want of bal-ance between the sexes—we are forced to regard all the ex-ogamous races as having originally been polyandrous. While polyandry supplied a method whereby the want of balance might be the less felt, and may thus have retarded, and in some cases prevented, the establishment of exogamy, wherever exogamy took root polyandry must have been practised. There-fore we must hold it to be beyond dispute that among exog-amous races the first system of kinship was that which recog-nised blood-ties through mothers only.

We may be pardoned for here adverting to the views of ancient kinship advanced by Mr. Maine. We have already pointed out[66] that Mr. Maine seems not to have been able to conceive of any social order more primitive than the patriarchal. And as he found agnation—or kinship exclusively through males—to be a common concomitant of the patriarchal system, he has committed himself to the opinion that that was the only kinship known to primitive times. He argues, indeed, against the possibility of kinship through females in early times as being inconsistent with social order and stability. The learned and ingenious writer must be held to have taken up the threads of legal history where they began to unwind themselves, of new, after the completion of a social revolution. It is quite undoubted, as he says, that few indigenous bodies of law be-longing to communities of the Indo-European stock do not exhibit peculiarities which are referable to agnation.[67] With the advance of society—the growth of marriage laws—the su-periority of the male sex must have everywhere tended to establish that system. But, before that result could be reached, many stages of progress had to be traversed. And while traces of agnation are to be found in the early customs of most of the

66. *Ante*, p. 48.
67. See *post*, p. 94.

Indo-European races, we have seen that the indigenous customs of most early communities—whether of the Indo-European, Turanian, or Semitic race—exhibit peculiarities intelligible only on the supposition that kinship and succession through females were the rule before the rise of agnation. Farther, we have seen that wherever non-advancing communities are to be found—isolated in islands or maintaining their savage liberties in mountain fastnesses—there to this day exists the system of kinship through females only. The state of old, says Mr. Maine, recognised as its units not individuals, but families. True. But at a yet older date we must conclude that neither the state, nor the family, properly speaking, existed. And at that earlier time the unnamed species of kinship—the counterpart and complement of agnation—was the chief determinant of social phenomena.

We now go on to show—

II.—*That the primitive groups were, or were assumed to be, homogeneous.*

It appeared at the outset that individuals must have been primarily affiliated not to persons but to groups, and that the first effect of the rise of the idea of kinship must have been to give birth to the conception of stocks; farther, that the establishment over any great area of the system of kinship through females only must have occupied a considerable period of time. Until that system was firmly established, there could be no such interference with the homogeneity of the groups as to be worth consideration. An amount of heterogeneity short of that which would introduce at least the *germ* of a system of betrothals may fairly be overlooked. While as yet there was no system of kinship, the presence of captive women in a horde, in whatever numbers, could not introduce a system of betrothals. Heterogeneity as a statical force can only have come into play when a system of kinship led the hordes to look on the children of their foreign women as belonging to the stocks of their mothers; that is, when the sentiments which grew up with the system of kinship became so strong as to overmaster the old filiation to the group (and its stock) of the children born within it. We may depend upon it that this was a stage of progress which it took long to reach, and thus that it was long before the original homogeneity of the groups was substantially impaired. That in the stage of progress we are contemplating, adoption was practised (the adoption of one group by another to which some writers ascribe such great effects), is altogether unlikely. If it was, it would most probably—as in later times— proceed on the fiction that the uniting groups were of the same original stock. But looking to the state of hostility between groups at the stage we are considering, and the degree of advancement implied in the conception of adoption, we cannot believe that the groups then tended to amalgamate, however they may have tended to divide. We conclude that we must regard the primitive groups as having been, or having been assumed to be, homogeneous up to that stage when, through the joint operation of exogamy and the system of kinship through females only, foreigners recognised as such began to be systematically born within them.

III.—*The system of kinship through females only tended to render the exogamous groups heterogeneous, and thus to supersede the system of capturing wives.*

We may here be very brief. We have already seen[68] the effects of the joint operation of exogamy and this system of kinship among the Australians. Indeed, what their effects must have been is exceedingly obvious. Owing to exogamy, the mothers in each horde were foreigners, and, owing to the system of kinship, the children born to them were esteemed foreigners also. Thus, so far as the system of infanticide allowed, the hordes contained young men and women accounted of different stocks, who might intermarry consistently with exogamy. Hence grew up a system of betrothals, and of marriage by sale and purchase. In Australia and America we saw that in spite of the law of blood-feud, the heterogeneity is now such that the system of betrothals is well established, and that of the original stock-groups the names alone appear to remain.

IV.—*As civilization advanced, the system of kinship through*

68. *Ante*, p. 49.

93

*females only was succeeded by a system which acknowledged
kinship through males also; and which in most cases passed into
a system which acknowledged kinship through males only.*

It is obviously needless to say anything in support of the
first branch of this proposition. The difficulty was to show, as
we have done in our first proposition in this chapter, that there
was a more archaic system which did not acknowledge kinship
through males. With the fact of kinship through males in advanced communities, every reader is familiar. Farther, as to
the second branch of the proposition, it is unnecessary to adduce evidence, or to do more than give some explanations.
Those who are acquainted with Mr. Maine's (in many respects
admirable) chapter on primitive society and ancient law, will
see from the terms of our proposition, that we have not altogether adopted his view that agnation at one time or other prevailed everywhere in the advancing communities; but it is beyond dispute that its prevalence was most general. As it will
be convenient hereafter to speak of agnation as a familiar system, we must here say something of its nature. This system,
as it long prevailed in Rome, may be best explained by using
the terminology of Roman Jurisprudence—to which indeed its
name belongs. Its general description is that it embraced only
the ties of blood through males. But it will be well to see who
were thus included in the kindred. Those united by ties of
blood through descent from the same married pair being called
cognates; the agnates were those cognates who traced their
connection exclusively through males. By a fiction, adopted
persons and their descendants through males were within the
agnatic bond. All the children of a married pair were agnates,
as well as all the grandchildren through sons, but the grandchildren through daughters were not in the number of agnates.
The children of the same father by different mothers were
kindred, but the children of the same mother by different
fathers were not relations to any legal effect. The sons of
brothers were kinsmen, but the sons of sisters or of brother
and sister were no relations; for a woman's children were held
to be not of the kin of their mother but of their father. And
in no case was there a tie of kinship between a woman's chil-

dren and her natural relatives unless there was an affinity between her and her husband. It is needless to say that the cognates who remain over, after deducting the agnates, are those
who would be relatives under the system of kinship through
females only. If the one system involved anomalies so did also
the other. Where female kinship prevails, a Rajah's son may
become a hodman—taking the state of his mother—while the
son of the Rajah's sister mounts the throne. The nephew—a
sister's child—is a relation of the Rajah, but his son is none at
all. No more is his brother's son; for through a male under that
system there is no blood-tie.

Under each system, while it prevailed, the effects of kinship
were confined to those who according to it were relations. And
often it is in the laws of succession that we find the best evidence of the former existence among a race of either system.
The rule preserved in the customs of Normandy, which prohibited uterine brothers from succeeding to one another's lands,
attests the former prevalence there of agnation; and, in some
quarters, as in Congo, the descent of the crown from the uncle
to the sister's son is nearly all that remains to witness to the
former prevalence of the system of kinship through females.
It will be a curious chapter in history which successfully nar-
rates the progress of the revolution by which the passage from
the earlier to the later of these systems was effected; exhibiting
the stages in the development of the family system, as based
upon the patria-potestas, and of agnatic kinship as deduced
therefrom.

Let us see whether we cannot in a few sentences suggest
some of the steps in that progress. The reader must suppose
the progress to commence as soon as, through the joint operation of exogamy and the system of female kinship, the groups
have been rendered so far heterogeneous as to permit of marriage within the group.

Children having been affiliated to mothers instead of to
groups, the first approach to a family system would be through
a separation of residences—all of a group having no longer a
common haunt or dwelling, but at first all of the same stock
within a group associating as a gens or house; and next, mothers

and their children occupying separate homes. With this separation of residences would come a closer knitting together of the kindred first in the gens, and next of mothers and children in the family—rude proprietary rights distinct from the tribal, distinct from the gentile—in the common home, weapons, and garnered food. There would be introduced such a species of family system as we find among the Nairs—the rudest that can be imagined. And from this to the family system, peculiar to polyandry of the Tibetan type, we have seen the stages of development.

In the Nair stage, kinship would be of importance chiefly in two respects—(1), as determining the right of intermarriage; (2), as determining the right of succession. It might be expected that the system of kinship through females only would first lose importance in regard to successions.

While the Nair family system lasted, we may assume that the common home of the brothers and mother would not often be such as to permit (conveniently) of a general succession—failing the brothers—of all the sister's children, where there was more than one sister; and that the first advance to a restricted system of succession would be through the limitation of the right of succession, *primo loco,* to the children of the eldest sister. We have seen the practice[69] growing of fathers making gifts, *inter vivos,* to women's children whom they had reason to think their own; and as this practice grew with the number of cases in which there was a degree of certainty of male parentage, there would be a farther practical restriction of the right of succession through females. And with the practice of gifts, *inter vivos,* to putative children, would grow a feeling against allowing estates to pass from the house of the brothers to that of, or to the putative children of, the polyandrous husbands of their sister, and a corresponding disposition towards a system of marriage which would allow of the property passing to the brother's own children. The system which would suggest itself would be the Tibetan system—to have a wife in common in the house of their mother. This system would produce cer-

69. *Ante,* p. 86.

tainty of the children being of their own blood; they would be born in the house, and would become its heirs.

The next step in advance is obvious. The succession of the younger brother to the elder was a feature of the earliest law —sister's sons only succeeded failing their uncles. Now, everything conspired to invest the eldest brother, when he came into the succession, with some of the attributes of a paterfamilias. This he did only on the death of all the polyandrous fathers. But—in his relation to his younger brothers—in respect of his being the first to marry, reaching puberty first, and choosing the future wife of himself and brothers—in respect of the first-born, and frequently more than one of the children of his marriage being unquestionably his offspring—it was natural that the fiction should be formed that *his* were all the children. Women had already, and in the recourse to Tibetan polyandry, been deposed from the sovereignty and management of families; and now, with additional guarantees for the wife's fidelity, parentage was either become certain, or feigned to be so; the elder brother was a sort of paterfamilias, the right to succeed him being in his younger brothers in their order; after them, in their eldest son. Thus, the idea of fatherhood—formed under the system of Nair polyandry—attained something like maturity under the Tibetan, and took its place in customary law. And so far as it was a step towards, or accompanied by kinship through males, it was a step away from kinship through females, and especially as regards rights of succession.

Apart from such certainty of fatherhood as was incidental to the marriage of eldest sons, the earliest examples of such married life as would give certainty of male parentage would probably be furnished by the chiefs of tribes, who might have the power to secure to themselves one, or perhaps several wives. In Kandya, Ceylon, where polyandry is universal among the lower and middle classes, the chiefs are strictly monogamists, apparently regarding polyandry as a low practice, unworthy of men in their position. As settled habits arose, as property accumulated, and the sexes became more evenly balanced, the example of the chiefs would find more and more imitators, and their cases would furnish a model for an improved system of succession. Thus would arise a practice of monogamy or of polygamy. Brothers would not now always be co-husbands; the Tibetan form of polyandry would die out, and the marriage of a brother to his elder brother's widow would become first an act of succession necessary for the assumption of the brother's place as head of the family; next, as the succession of sons was introduced as in right prior to the brother of a father—chiefly through the brothers leaving the house and contracting separate marriages—it would become an obligation founded on usage, and which, being unproductive of material advantages, would not unfrequently, from men's other marriages, be found irksome and inconvenient. Finally, the obligation itself would die out under the influence of ideas of propriety, which grew up with the improved marriage system. In the Institutes of Menu the obligation is seen in a state of decadence under the influence of such ideas.

Paternity having become certain, a system of kinship through males would arise with the growth of property, and a practice of sons succeeding, as heirs direct, to the estates of fathers; and as the system of kinship through males arose, that through females would—and chiefly under the influence of property—die away. The cases of Abraham and Nahor, however, show that it would be long before that system ceased to be influential as regards intermarriages; that it might, as regards them, linger to some effect even after men had reached the patriarchal state. From the patriarchal state, with such a customary law as prevailed in Abraham's time, to the system of agnation as it prevailed in Rome, is still a long progress. Every step in it, we may be sure, was affected by considerations derived from property. While wives were captured, if there was any sense of property at all, wives would be regarded as property. When at a later stage they came to pass from the houses of their birth into alien houses—by purchase—they would still be property. And with the wives considered as property, it is easy to conceive how there would have arisen a sense of property in children. Hence, additional features of the patria potestas. And when a woman had been *sold* to her husband by her father, and had thus come to be considered the husband's property, it is easy to see how neither her original family, nor that into which she had married, should be able to inherit any property through her. But the right of inheritance, as property became abundant, tended to become, and did become, the test of kinship. And in course of time, the notion of kinship derived through females would disappear among a people who cared nothing for a kinship barren as regarded patrimonial advantages. The result would be the system of agnation.

It is not necessary for us here to do more than repeat that we have, in numerous cases, found agnation, or at least kinship through males, preceded by the system of kinship through females only. It was so in the cases of the Hebrews, Hindus, Celts, and Greeks; it was presumably so in all those cases in which we find kinship through males accompanied by that relic of polyandry—the obligation laid on younger brothers in turn to marry the widow of the elder brother deceased. And since we have shown special cause for believing that all the exogamous races had originally the system of kinship through females only, we are entitled to assume that it was so among those exogamous peoples with which, as with the Khonds, the Circassians, and the Kalmucks, we find relationship to be agnatic.

V.—*The system of kinship through males tended to rear up homogeneous groups, and thus to restore the original condition of affairs among exogamous races, as regards both the practice of capturing wives and the evolution of the form of capture.*

The first effect of kinship through males must have been to arrest the progress of heterogeneity. The introduction of foreign women into a tribe no longer brought into it children accounted foreigners; for either the children were no longer of the mother's stock, but of the father's, or, if of the mother's, they were yet of the father's also. Where, then, in a tribe, a balance of persons of different stocks had not been reached, it was henceforth unattainable. Farther, with kinship through males would arise the habit of feigning a common descent from some distinguished man—a fiction which would lead in many cases to the denial or neglect of such heterogeneity as existed. Of the new groups that were formed, the homogeneity was perfectly

secured. The family now tended to grow into the tribe of kinsfolk. The children born to a polygamist husband were all kinsfolk, of whatever stocks their mothers were. The children of
brothers, though they married women of different stocks, were
kinsfolk. And however the family increased by the addition of
generations, its members were all within the kindred. And that,
as well where the exogamous prejudice survived as where it
perished. Where it survived the women of a family could find
no mates within its bounds, and marrying into other groups
would follow, and their children with them, the kindred of
their husbands. They would be out of the group. Thus, within
such exogamous groups as were remodelled, and within such
new exogamous groups as were formed, under this species of
kinship there could be no marriage within the group. There
would be no place for a system of betrothals; and except where
friendly relations subsisted between the groups to allow of
marriage by purchase, their members would once more be able
to get wives only by capturing them. Thus, even if, in the first
stage, the system of capture had—as we see in Australia that
it partially has—been superseded, the exogamous races, in entering on a new phase of advancement, had reserved for them
a farther experience of that system, to confirm or re-establish
the old association between marriage and the act of rapine. And
we cannot doubt that many exogamous peoples have had this
twofold experience. We know of several exogamous races
which, after having had kinship through females, had kinship
through males; and we cannot doubt that the same was the
case with the other exogamous races that have had the form
of capture and agnatic relationship. And indeed, as in the later
stage, the experience must have been more uniform and con-
tinuous, there being nothing, in the absence of friendliness between the groups, to interfere with the system of capture, so
it is observable that the form of capture is now most distinctly
marked and impressive just among those races which have
male kinship. It might be doubted, but for the case of the
Fuegians and traces of the symbol, as if of a thing decayed,
occurring in America, whether the experience of the earlier

stage could generate the form. There is no doubt it can, and has frequently done so; but the question whether it could have done so, might, on mere general reasoning, have been decided in the negative.

VI.—*Under the combined influence of exogamy and the system of female kinship, a local tribe might attain a balance of persons regarded as being of different descent, and its members might thus be able to intermarry with one another, and wholly within the tribe, in consistency with the principle of exogamy.*

This sufficiently appears from what has preceded; and it farther appears from what has preceded, that such a balance of the sexes as would render a group independent of other groups in the matter of marriage would more speedily be reached in respect of the practice of polyandry.

VII.—*A local tribe having reached the stage contemplated in the last proposition, and having grown proud through successes in war, might become a caste.*

It is obvious that the feeling of superiority to other tribes, concurring with independence of them as regards marriage, might lead a tribe first to avoid, and then to decline and prohibit, intermarriage with the tribes which it esteemed inferior. And a tribe with a marriage-law restricted by such a prohibition is a caste, or has made an approach towards being a caste. That castes have, in fact, been produced in this way, is rendered certain by the fact already referred to—that nearly all the Indian castes, from the highest to the lowest, are divided into gotrams or families, and that marriage is prohibited between persons of the same gotram, who, according to the rule of Menu, are shown by their common name to be of the same original stock. We hold that this at once shows the caste to have been composed of members of different original stocks, and the stocks themselves to have been originally exogamous. There can, we think, be little doubt that all castes of this description were formed by the processes which we have been explaining. The Kamilaroi among the Australians appear to be such a caste. And were the natives of Australia to be left to themselves, their system of kinship remaining what it is, we might expect hereafter to find among them numerous caste tribes of this description.[70]

It is a rider on what has preceded that caste may appear at that stage of a people's progress while they are yet polyandrous. And of caste among people at that stage we have several instances.

VIII.—*On kinship becoming agnatic, the members of a caste, formed as above explained, might—yielding to a common tendency of rude races—feign themselves to be all descended from a common ancestor, and thus become endogamous.*

On the appearance of kinship through males, much confusion must for a time have prevailed in the application of the principle of exogamy. Some marriages that were formerly allowable would become illegal: as, for instance, the marriage of brother and sister-german, or of the children of brothers; on the other hand, some marriages that were before illegal would become allowable, as for instance the marriages of sisters' children. At least the marriages last mentioned would be consistent with exogamy where relationship became agnatic. And as the old rules thus became inapplicable new rules would be formed, which in some cases might ignore the principle upon which the old proceeded. At any rate it is manifest that, while the application of the principle in the new circumstances was *in dubio,* the fiction of a common descent from an illustrious ancestor, should it be put forward, would come in aid of the confusion to destroy or render obsolete the principle of exogamy. The members of the caste already restricted to marriages among themselves, and now feigning themselves all to be kindred, would become endogamous.

70. It is worth mentioning that many of the rude caste tribes in the hills of India,—such as the Kocch,—have the blood-tie through mothers only. Whether marriage is subject to any, or what, restrictions within these caste tribes, we have no information. The reader will understand that, in speaking of castes, we distinguish between castes proper—the divisions of a people as determined by the right of intermarriage—and the classical subdivisions of castes proper, which are often met with, and which are also frequently called castes. We believe with Dr. Roth that the division into classes resulted from the growth and establishment of professions, and was of later date than the division into castes proper.

Indeed, all that is necessary for the production of an endogamous tribe is, that a caste tribe composed of members of different stocks should, anyhow, at any time, yield to the tendency to eponymy. We see, however, that in the stage of transition from the system of female kinship to agnation, or to a system of male kinship, there must have been a time highly favourable for the introduction of the fiction of a common descent, and of the destruction thereby of exogamy. Of the tendency of rude races to employ that fiction, it is unnecessary that we should say anything; it is familiar to all students of early history. Nothing is more common than to find the belief in a common descent among peoples obviously heterogeneous; sometimes the belief is found even in communities which are not only heterogeneous, but the composition of which is known to be entirely artificial.[71]

And if we anywhere find the form of capture among an endogamous race, as we do among the Bedouin Arabs, and appear to do among the Hebrews, it is not, we think, too much to say that the presence of the form is confirmatory of the supposition that the race became endogamous through employing this fiction, and by the processes which we have been explaining. At least this is the only explanation which we can offer of the appearance among an endogamous people of the form of capture.[72]

We have now gone over the ground laid out at the close of the last chapter. It will be seen that some of the propositions mutually support one another. For example, the observed heterogeneity of certain castes which are subject to the rule of exogamy, goes to show that their ancestors must have had the

71. "Ancient Law," 1861, p. 263.
72. As to the unity of physical characteristics observed in most castes, we notice that even in the stage when exogamy is yet observed, they were, owing to their intermarriages and the close connections permitted by a system of kinship which ignored half of the natural blood-ties, steadily advancing to one type, as consanguinii. Where the caste became properly endogamous the circumstances were only just more favourable to the production of that type. There is nothing in the observed unity discordant with the assumption of original heterogeneity; nothing, especially when we consider the periods of time at our disposal, to allow for the production of a uniform type among a people strictly limited to marriages among themselves.

system of kinship through females only; for exogamy, by itself, will not explain the welding together, in a group, of persons of different original stocks. And to those who, from the earlier chapters, have formed the opinion that we are right in our theory of the origin of the form of capture, the appearance of the form among an endogamous race will strengthen the supposition that many endogamous races, which have not—or which we do not know to have—the form, may originally have been exogamous.

We may fitly close this chapter with some surmises—thrown out for what they are worth—as to some of the effects on early society of the law of blood-feud which exists everywhere, so far as we know, among rude races, and which of course grew up with, and out of kinship. So far as the law of blood-feud retarded the production of heterogeneity within the groups in any district, it was unfriendly to progress. From another point of view it appears that it must have favoured progress, especially among exogamous races, at that stage when kinship was through females only. It bound all the kindred to avenge the death of any one, and the obligation was a point of religion. At first, probably, the protection to the person which this law afforded may have extended only to adults, but in time it came to be extended even to infants. This extension indeed was a logical necessity. And when infants came within the benefit of the law, their lives must often have been spared to avoid the blood-feud with their mother's kindred—a body of protectors, as we have seen, usually living outside and foreign to the gens or house of birth. Thus the law of blood-feud must be credited with a mitigation, perhaps in some cases with the suppression, of infanticide, male as well as female, in exogamous societies, at that stage when kinship is through mothers only. And by checking this practice it tended to restore the balance of the sexes, to allow of the rise of polygunia and the decay of polyandry. It is a curious fact that nowhere now, that we are aware of, is infanticide *a system* where exogamy and the earliest form of kinship co-exist.

When, however, with agnation, groups became homogeneous, containing none but kindred, and containing in fact all *the* kindred, this beneficial action of the blood-feud must have ceased. Where necessity or convenience prompted to infanticide among agnatic groups, the law of blood-feud opposed no impediment to the practice. If the children perished it was at the hands of their kindred. Accordingly the most impressive *systems* of infanticide—chiefly systems of female infanticide—now existing, occur among exogamous races which have male kinship.

On the one hand, then, the law of blood-feud would seem to have played an important part in introducing monogamy, polygunia, and the patriarchal system; on the other hand, it would seem at a later stage to have favoured the perpetuation of exogamy, and of systems of infanticide.

9

The Decay of Exogamy in Advancing Communities

IT will complete the view of early society, to which we have been led by our investigation of the origin of the form of capture, if we point out the principal causes of the breakdown of exogamy in advancing communities. We have seen the liability of the principle to decay in the confusion incident to the growth of the system of kinship through males; and have found reason to think that it gave place to endogamy in many tribes which had, previous to the revolution in kinship, nearly attained a balance—sufficient for the purposes of marriage—of persons accounted of different stocks. It remains, then, that we should consider the causes of the neglect of the principle where it perished gradually, and without the people becoming endogamous.

To indicate the causes in any case will be sufficient for our purpose. We select the cases of Greece and Rome as being those which, to the generality of readers, are most familiar. That the Greeks and the Romans were originally exogamous may be inferred from three distinct grounds, separately, and in combination. (1), They present us with the Form of Capture in marriage ceremonies. (2), Many of their mythic traditions are incapable of a rational explanation, except on the hypothesis that they anciently had the system of capturing women for wives. (3), The composition and organization of their tribes and commonwealths cannot well be explained, except on the hypothesis that they resulted from the joint operation, in early times, of exogamy, and the system of kinship through females only. The two first grounds we have already noticed; on the third, we must now dwell somewhat. It not only affords new evidence of the prevalence of exogamy, but introduces us to the chief causes of its decay in advancing communities.

The old theory of the composition of States, was based upon

the tendency of families to multiply round a central family, whose head represented the original progenitor of them all. The family, under the government of a father, was assumed to be the primary group—the elementary social unit; in it were found at once the germs of the State, and of sovereign authority. Many circumstances recommended this theory, and none more than its apparent simplicity. It was easy to find abundant analogies for the prolongation of the family into the State. A family tends to multiply families around it, till it becomes the centre of a tribe, just as the banyan tends to surround itself with a forest of its own offshoots. And it is obvious, to follow up this figure, by remarking that the feelings of kindred which hold families together in tribes, tend to bind together, in nations, tribes which, like the Greek races, trace back their descent to kinsmen.

The origin of the State on this view is so simple, that a child may comprehend it. But it is very easily shown that the theory cannot be supported. In the first place, it is not borne out by history. The tribes are numerous whose members claim to be descended from a common progenitor. Inquiry, however, everywhere discloses the fact, that the common progenitor is a fiction—a hero or god, called into being to explain the tribe—from whom the tribe did not derive its being. In many cases, not only the fact that the genealogy is fictitious, but even the time when it was invented, can be shown;[1] and nowhere can tribes or nations be traced back to individuals. Also, the theory turns on a fundamental error as to the primitive state. It postulates that human history opens with perfect marriage, conjugal fidelity, and certainty of male parentage—that, from the first, all the necessary conditions of the rise of a perfect family system were satisfied. Demonstrably, history did not so begin; and hence, demonstrably, the family—the social unit of the theory—is not the primary unit it is assumed to be. Farther, and apart from these objections, the theory is wanting in this essential quality of a good theory, viz., that it should explain, or be capable of being made to appear to explain, the facts.

1. This can be done in regard to the Greek races which traced their descent to the sons of Helen.

The more acute thinkers who have adopted it, and who at the same time have rejected, as they felt constrained to do, the principle of contiguity, as a principle on which groups in early times united,[2] have discerned serious difficulties in the way of entertaining the theory. Mr. Maine especially seems to have been impressed with these difficulties, and to have been unable to find any proper solution of them.

"In most of the Greek States, and in Rome," says Mr. Maine,[3]

> there long remained vestiges of an ascending series of groups, out of which the State was at first constituted. The family, house, and tribe of the Romans, may be taken as the type of them; and they are so described to us, that we can scarcely help conceiving them as a system of concentric circles, which have gradually expanded from the same point. The elementary group is the family connected by common subjection to the highest male ascendant. The aggregation of families (which elsewhere[4] he calls the fictitious extension of the family) forms the gens or house. The aggregation of houses makes the tribe. The aggregation of tribes forms the commonwealth.

Obviously, this is not an explanation of the growth of the commonwealth. It does not show how, consistently with the assumption of the family as the elementary unit, the various aggregations spoken of were effected. The gens, clan, or house, which occurs in early tribes wherever we look, was in India, Greece, and Rome, as elsewhere, composed of all the persons in the tribe (included in families, of course), bearing the same name, and accounted of the same stock. Were the gentes really of different stocks, as their names would imply, and as the people believed? If so, how came clans of different stocks to be united in the same tribe? The production of a tribe of one stock—of a homogeneous agnatic group—is readily conceivable

2. Aristotle kept clear of many of the difficulties which surround the theory of the derivation of the state from the family, by making the combination of families of different stocks depend on contiguity of residence, and on convenience.

3. "Ancient Law," p. 128.

4. P. 200.

on the family hypothesis. But how came a variety of such groups—of different stocks—to coalesce in a local tribe? On the other hand, how came a tribe of descent to be divided into clans situated in different local tribes; how came such a tribe to be at all divided into clans or houses?

To these questions no proper answer has, so far as we know, been given. The common supposition is, that the heterogeneity of the local tribes was somehow brought about by the fiction of adoption. It is supposed that the agnatic groups must have united through this fiction, the one adopting the other on the pretence of kinship; although, after their union, they preserved their distinctive names. Mr. Maine does not expressly say that the observed combination of heterogeneous elements in tribes, and hence in the commonwealth—often assumed to be composed wholly of kindred—was due to the employment of the fiction of adoption; but he leaves that conclusion to be drawn by his readers. "If," he says, "adoption had never existed, I do not see how any one of the primitive groups (*i.e.*, the agnatic brotherhoods, for he contemplates none other), whatever were their nature, could have absorbed one another; or, on what terms any two of them could have combined, except those of absolute superiority on the one side, and absolute subjection on the other." Here the difficulty is distinctly perceived; but, is it overcome? What is the evidence that the fiction of adoption was ever employed on so grand a scale as we must suppose, to explain the heterogeneity of such groups as the tribes of Rome, Greece, or India? We say that there is none. It is a case of error, induced by the maxim "causa aequat effectum." As the fiction of adoption was the only cause conceived of, that might have produced the observed phenomena, it has been assumed to have been employed on the scale required by its supposed effects. But, we repeat, there is no evidence that it was so employed. And there is no likelihood that it was so employed. Our belief is, that adoption has been much more extensively employed by philosophers to explain, than it was by rude races to produce, heterogeneity. It is of no consequence how families and gentes were adulterated by the practice of adoption. The difficulty to be got over does not lie so much in any want of

purity of the so-called stocks, as in the union of different stocks
—admittedly different—in the same tribe.

The phenomena we have been contemplating offer no difficulty when regarded from the point of view to which we have
been led by our investigation. To satisfy the reader of this, we
must to some extent recapitulate. We started in the last chapter
from the conception of populations, the units of which were
homogeneous groups or tribes, which, on the introduction of
kinship, became the stock groups of each particular district or
country, and gave their names to the variety of stocks subsequently known to the district or country. And we saw how,
into the groups, and into their sections, if they divided, exogamy conjointly with the system of kinship through females
only, while it endured, systematically imported strangers, and
thus in time rendered the groups heterogeneous, and the general population to the same[5] extent homogeneous. We saw how
thus every local tribe came to consist of persons of different
stocks; also how all of the same stock, in each, were bound
together by rights and obligations springing out of kinship; and
how they were also united—though to less practical effect—
to all others of the same stock in whatever local tribes residing.
Farther, we saw that, when kinship became agnatic, the character of the local tribes became stereotyped, the causes of
heterogeneity ceasing to operate.

In each local tribe all the men of the same stock and name
were bound by kinship to common action, in certain cases,
against the men of other stocks, both in the tribe and elsewhere.
Here we have the gentes in the local tribe. And gentes of the
same stock and name would exist in different neighbouring
local tribes. We shall learn from this how the causes which led
to the diffusion of the stocks throughout the population, favoured the union of the population in the commonwealth. Most
probably contiguous tribes would be composed of precisely the
same stocks—would contain gentes of precisely the same names,
and thus be in the strictest sense akin—kindred. There is no
difficulty in conceiving equal unions taking place between such

5. That is to the same *recognised* extent, but really to a much greater,
half the blood-ties being overlooked.

tribes under the influence of kinship, similarity of elements and structure, contiguity and convenience. And on the union of several local tribes under a common government, the gentes of each stock in the combination would be recognised as forming together *a tribe of descent*, as in reality they would do. Thus, the tribes of descent in the commonwealth would each embrace several gentes which had taken shape, and acquired special rights and property in the local tribes in which they respectively were, before the union in the State. As the gens (or the germ thereof) would arise under the influence of female kinship, it would precede—probably long precede—agnatic kinship and the family system as they existed in Rome. And we have already seen something of the processes by which the gentes would be resolved into rude family groups, and the family system gradually advance into the patriarchal, till the gentes would be resolved into a series of families of the Roman type. The order of social development, in our view, is then, that the tribe stands first; the gens or house next; and last of all, the family. We are satisfied that the more the reader studies the phenomena of early tribal composition—the phratries and such-like unions of persons in different tribes—the more he will be convinced that this was the order of the genesis of tribes, gentes, and families; and that in no other way can the phenomena of the composition of early states be satisfactorily explained.[6]

Assuming that we have given the true account of the origin of clans of different names and stocks in local tribes, and of the appearance of distinct houses of the same name in tribes

6. We recommend to the reader a perusal of the Translator's Preface to the Oxford translation (1830) of C. O. Müller's "History and Antiquities of the Doric Race"—the translators being Henry Tufnell and Sir George Cornewall Lewis. If the reader keeps in view that we have good evidence of the existence at one time of the system of kinship through females only among the Dorians, we believe he will not be able to peruse the passage of Dicaearchus translated in that preface, and the Editor's comments thereon, without being strongly impressed that our views are the only views on which the phenomena of early Doric communities can be made intelligible. And if he farther study Chap. x., Part ii. of Mr. Grote's "History of Greece," we believe his impression of the correctness of our views will be deepened.

of descent, in ancient commonwealths, we might greatly extend the area of exogamy. But to do so is not our present purpose. We observe that the breakdown of exogamy in advancing communities must have been most intimately connected with this evolution of clans and families, and of clan and family estates within the tribe. As we have already had occasion to point out, the only species of property known anywhere originally appears to have been property in common. Everywhere it would appear that the groups were at the first the only owners. And the history of the right of property, as we have it, is just that of the growth *inside* groups of proprietary rights distinct from the tribal. It was an advance when clan estates were recognised as distinct from the tribal; it was a farther advance when family estates were recognised as distinct from those of the clan. Barbarism was already far in the rear when individual property made its appearance.

Now, when the authentic history of Rome begins, marriage-laws had not only become stringent, but modern in character, conjugal fidelity had become common, and, as the consequence, relationship had become agnatic. The tribal system, moreover, had been stripped of several of its leading features. Property had long been localized in families as distinct from gentes; and this localization had cut the families off from one another, and to a large extent from the gentes. Families were still associated in gentes; the gentes in tribes, for political purposes; and there remained to the gentiles the right and *spes successionis* to family estates, failing legitimate heirs. But already the laws of succession which had sprung up with family property—which were springing up with individual property—were training the people to consider a few persons only as their kinsmen in any special sense. And the course of decadence of the recognition of extended kinships in Greece followed much the same path. However strongly implanted the principle of exogamy may have originally been, it must have succumbed to the influences which thus disintegrated the old bonds of kinship. So complete was the disintegration, that in Rome while the right of succession still remained in the gentiles as evidence of kinship, and its rights and obligations, having been originally coextensive

112

with the gens, we find this so far lost sight of in the nebulosities of legal terminology, that the lawyers declared that all consanguinity ended with their names for its seven degrees—names invented with a view to the regulation of successions; ended there, "quia ulterius per rerum naturam nec nomina inveniri nec vita succedentibus prorogari potest." [7] A maxim, by the way, which proved very convenient to those pontiffs who maintained that the Levitical rule prohibited marriage between all blood relations, and which is probably found very convenient now in Russia where the Greek church still asserts that view of the Levitical rule. For the rest, it must be enough to say that exogamy died out with the blood-ties on which its existence depended, and that the process of destruction of those ties which the laws of succession inaugurated, was carried on and completed by the law of Testaments. If to this general view anything should be added, perhaps it is that the earliest violations of the rule of exogamy would appear to have been called for in the case of female heiresses. Such ladies, if they made proper marriages according to old law—at that stage of progress when a wife was usually what they call in Ceylon a deega wife, *i.e.*, passed from her own family into the family and village of her husband—must have carried their estates into other tribes or gentes, and so have cut off their own gentiles from the prospect of succeeding them. Numbers xxxvi contains an account of the origin among the Israelites of the rule prohibiting a female heiress from marrying out of the tribe of the family of her father. And the prohibition is not uncommon.

7. Paulus, Senten. Recept., Lib. iv., Tit ii.

10

Conclusion

HERE our argument ends. Apparently simple as was the
problem to be solved, it has now received a solution for
the first time. That solution opens a new series of problems
for the consideration of the philosopher; of some of which,
indeed, we have offered solutions, which, in the fervour of the
first conception, may have been put forward in too sanguine
a spirit. It will be something, however, if, in proposing and
trying to solve such problems, we have at least succeeded in
showing their importance, by displaying them on the level of
the foundations of civil society. The chief of these questions
respect the origin of exogamy and of endogamy. As to the
origin of the former, it will be remarked that we have not
spent time on the consideration of the question, whether it
may not have been due to a natural feeling against the union
of near kinsfolk. Its general description might dispose one to
think that it might have been due to such a feeling. But, owing
to the nature of ancient kinship, as we have seen it, exogamy
afforded no proper security against the intermixture of persons
near of kin. It permitted, in reality, many marriages which we
now disallow. Ties of blood that were not recognised—though
that they were ties of blood must have been vaguely perceived
—were practically nonexistent. And, in the first stages of human development, it was agreeable to exogamy that brothers
and sisters of the half-blood should marry, while uncles might
marry nieces, and nephews aunts. Afterwards, unions equally
incestuous, as we should say, were allowable in consequence
of the limitation in blood-ties derived from agnation. One thing
is very clear, that in ancient times such questions as have been
raised by modern science, as to the propriety of the marriages
of near relatives, were never considered. On the whole, the
account which we have given of the origin of exogamy, appears
the only one which will bear examination. The scarcity of
women within the group led to a practice of stealing the women

of other groups, and in time it came to be considered improper, because it was unusual, for a man to marry a woman of his own group. Another important question respects the universality of kinship through females only. The strong *a priori* presumptions in favour of that, as the most archaic system of kinship, backed by so much evidence as we have been able to adduce, seem to us satisfactorily to establish the position which we have taken up. On the other hand, much labour and investigation will yet be needed to show clearly that that kinship was not merely a concomitant of exogamy and polyandry, should cases occur in which it must be held that neither polyandry nor exogamy was primitive custom. Assuming the universality of that kinship, the question remains: What were the stages of development of the family system, founded on the principle of agnation, as at Rome? Some of these questions we have grappled with; at others we have done little more than glance. Are we too sanguine if we venture to predict that their solution will yet be reached, and will exhibit early human history in a very different light from that in which it has hitherto been regarded, by what Dugald Stewart calls "that indolent philosophy which refers to a miracle whatever appearance both in the natural and moral worlds it is unable to explain"?

Appendix

Note A
Additional Examples of
the Form of Capture

It is to be remarked of the examples of the Form of Capture in the text, as of those which follow, that they have never before been collated or made the subject of serious speculation. They are just noted as matters of curiosity where they occur, the authorities venturing no explanation, except in one or two cases, of their meaning or origin; and only in some cases noticing similar customs as having prevailed elsewhere than in the district reported upon. They are thus presented to us in a trustworthy shape as materials for an induction. It may be added, as regards the additional examples of the Form of Capture here appended, that, like the examples in the text, they, with two exceptions, show that the central idea in the symbol was the carrying off of the woman, in defiance of her kindred and of their efforts to protect her. The first of the following examples of the form is in some respects the most striking of any of which we have an account.

1. "In their marriages," says Sir Henry Piers of the Irish, "especially in those countries where cattle abound, the parents and friends on each side meet on the side of an hill, or, if the weather be cold, in some place of shelter, about midway between both dwellings. If agreement ensue, they drink the agreement bottle, as they call it, which is a bottle of good usquebaugh, and this goes merrily round. For payment of the portion—which is generally a determinate number of cows—little care is taken. The father or next of kin to the bride sends to his neighbours and friends *sub mutuae vicissitudinis obtentu,* and every one gives his cow or heifer, and thus the portion is quickly paid. Nevertheless, caution is taken from the bridegroom on the day of delivery for restitution of the cattle, in case the bride die childless within a certain day, limited by agreement; and, in this case, every man's own beast is restored. Thus, care is taken that no man shall grow rich by frequent marriages. On the day of bringing home, the bridegroom and his friends ride out and meet the bride and her friends at the place of meeting. *Being come near each other,*

116

the custom was of old to cast short darts at the company that attended the bride, but at such distance that seldom any hurt ensued. Yet it is not out of the memory of man that the Lord of Hoath on such an occasion lost an eye. This custom of casting darts is now obsolete."—Vallencey's "Collectanea de Rebus Hibernicis," vol. i. p. 122, 1786, No. 1, Description of Westmeath, by Sir Henry Piers—written A.D. 1682.

2. We have an account from M. Huc of the constitution of marriage among the Mongols of the Ortous. After stating that marriage is with the Mongols a matter of sale and purchase; that this is clearly expressed, in their language, in such phrases as—"I have bought for my son the daughter of So-and-so"; "We have sold our daughter to such-and-such a family"; and that the lady for some time after the sale remains with her family, M. Huc proceeds to say that the day having arrived, "the bridegroom sends early in the morning a deputation to fetch the girl who has been betrothed to him, or rather whom he has bought. *When the envoys draw near, the relations and friends of the bride place themselves in a circle before the door, as if to oppose the departure of the bride, and then begins a feigned fight, which of course terminates in the bride being carried off.* She is placed on a horse, and having been thrice led round her paternal house, she is then taken at full gallop to the tent which has been prepared for the purpose, near the dwelling of her father-in-law. Meantime, all the Tartars of the neighbourhood, the relations and friends of both families, repair to the wedding-feast, and offer their presents to the newly-married pair."—Hazlitt's Translation of Huc's "Travels," vol. i. p. 185, illustrated library edition.

3. We find the following account of the constitution of marriage among the Toorkomans:—

"The most singular customs of these people (the Toorkomans) relate to marriage. The Toorkomans do not shut up their women, and there being no restraint on the social intercourse between the sexes, as in most Mussulman countries, love matches are common. A youth becomes acquainted with a girl; they are mutually attached, and agree to marry; but the young man does not dare to breathe his wishes to the parents of his beloved, for such is not etiquette, and would be resented as an insult. What does he do? He elopes with the girl and carries her to some neighbouring obah, where, such is the custom, there is no doubt of a kind reception; and there the young couple live as man and wife for some six weeks, when the Reish-suffeeds, or elders of the protecting obah, deem it time to talk over the matter with the parents. Accordingly they represent the wishes of the young couple, and, joined by the elders of the father's obah, endeavour to reconcile him to the union, promising on the part of the bridegroom, a handsome *bashlogue*, or price, for his wife. In due time the consent is given, on which the bride returns to her father's house, where, strange to say, she is retained for six months or a year, and sometimes two years, according, as it appears, to her caprice or the parent's will, having no communication with her husband, unless by stealth. The meaning of this strange separation I never could ascertain. . . . Afterwards the marriage presents and price of the wife are interchanged, and she goes finally to live with her husband."—Fraser's "Journey" (1838), vol. ii. p. 372.

"Matches are also made occasionally by the parents themselves, with or without the intervention of the Reish-suffeeds, but the order and ceremonies of the nuptials are the same. There is a regular contract and a stipulated price; the young people are permitted to enjoy each other's society for a month or six weeks; and the bride then returns, as in the former case, to spend a year or more with her parents."—*Idem.*, vol. ii. p. 375.

This case illustrates a stage of transition from the system of actual capture to a symbolism, of which stage traces remained in Sparta in historic times. In Sparta the young wife was not, immediately after the marriage, domiciled in her husband's house, but cohabited with him for some time clandestinely, till he brought her, and frequently her mother also, to his home. (Xenophon, Rep. Lac. 1–5.) And the same custom prevailed in Crete. (Strabo, x., p. 432.) In example No. 7 we shall again see these peculiarities in combination with the Form of Capture.

4. Among the Soligas (India), "when a girl consents to marry, the man runs away with her to some neighbouring village, and they live there until the honeymoon is over. They then return home, and give a feast to the people of their village."—Buchanan's "Journey from Madras," vol. ii. p. 178.

5. "The marriage ceremony is very simple among the Aenezes. . . . The marriage-day being appointed (usually five or six days after the betrothing), the bridegroom comes with a lamb in his arms to the tent of the girl's father, and there cuts the lamb's throat before witnesses. As soon as the blood falls upon the ground the marriage ceremony is regarded as complete. The men and girls amuse themselves with feasting and singing. Soon after sunset, the bride-

118

groom retires to a tent pitched for him at a distance from the camp; there he shuts himself up, and awaits the arrival of his bride. The bashful girl meanwhile runs from the tent of one friend to another till she is caught at last, and conducted in triumph by a few women to the bridegroom's tent; he receives her at the entrance, and forces her into it; the women who had accompanied her then depart."— Burckhardt's "Notes," vol. i. p. 107.

6. Burckhardt, after noticing that, among the Bedouins of Mount Sinai, marriage is a matter of sale and purchase, in which the in- clinations of the bride are not consulted, proceeds:—"Among the Arabs of Sinai the young maid comes home in the evening with the cattle. At a short distance from the camp she is met by the future spouse and a couple of his young friends, and carried off by force to her father's tent. If she entertains any suspicion of their designs, she defends herself with stones, and often inflicts wounds on the young men, even though she does not dislike the lover; for, accord- ing to custom, the more she struggles, bites, kicks, cries, and strikes, the more she is applauded ever after by her own companions." She is then taken to her father's tent. There follows the throwing over her of the abba, or man's cloak, and a formal announcement of the name of her future husband; after this she is dressed in bridal apparel, and mounted on a camel, "although still continuing to struggle in a most unruly manner, and held by the bridegroom's friends on both sides." She is led in this way to, and three times round, and finally into, the bridegroom's tent. The resistance is con- tinued till the last. The marriage, of course, ends in a feast, and presents to the bride.—Burckhardt's "Notes," vol. i. p. 263.

7. Among the Mezeyne, marriage appears to be a matter of sale and purchase, and to be constituted, as among the Aenezes, through capture as a form. It is attended, however, by a peculiar custom, which we have already met, though not in so striking a shape. "A singular custom," says Burckhardt ("Notes," vol. i. p. 269), "prevails among the Mezeyne tribe, within the limits of the Sinai peninsula, but not among the other tribes of that province. A girl having been wrapped in the abba at night (*i. e.*, after the capture as in the pre- ceding case), is permitted to escape from her tent and fly into the neighbouring mountains. The bridegroom goes in search of her next day, and remains often many days before he can find her out, while her female friends are apprised of her hiding-place, and furnish her with provisions. If the husband finds her at last (which is sooner or later, according to the impression that he has made upon the girl's

heart), he is bound to consummate the marriage in the open country, and to pass the night with her in the mountains. The next morning the bride goes home to her tent, that she may have some food; but again runs away in the evening, and repeats these flights several times, till she finally returns to her tent. She does not go to live in her husband's tent till she is far advanced in pregnancy; if she does not become pregnant she may not join her husband till after a full year from the wedding-day." Burckhardt says the same custom is observed among the Mezeyne Arabs elsewhere.

Appendix

Note B
On the Practice of
Capturing Wives

1. AN anonymous writer in "Chambers' Journal," October 22, 1864, gives the following account of the position of women, and of the practice of capturing wives, among the Australian Blacks. The writer would appear to have had good opportunities of being acquainted with the native customs:—

"In nothing is the brutality of their nature more clearly shown than in their treatment of their females. Amongst them, women are considered as an inferior class, and are used almost as beasts of burden; so that it is not at all uncommon to meet a huge black fellow travelling merrily along with no load but his spear or war-club, whilst his unfortunate *leubra* is panting under the weight of their goods and chattels, which she is compelled to carry from camp to camp. Courtship, as the precursor to marriage, is unknown amongst them. When a young warrior is desirous of procuring a wife, he generally obtains one by giving in exchange for her a sister, or some other female relative of his own; but if there should happen to be no eligible damsel disengaged in the tribe to which he belongs, then he hovers round the encampment of some other blacks until he gets an opportunity of seizing one of their leubras, whom perhaps he has seen and admired when attending one of the grand corroborries. His mode of paying his addresses is simple and efficacious. With a blow of his *nulla-nulla* (war-club), he stuns the object of his 'affections,' and drags her insensible body away to some retired spot, whence, as soon as she recovers her senses, he brings her home to his own gunyah in triumph. Sometimes two join in an expedition for the same purpose, and then for several days they watch the movements of their intended victims, using the utmost skill in concealing their presence. When they have obtained the knowledge they require, they wait for a dark, windy night; then quite naked, and carrying only their long 'jag-spears,' they crawl stealthily through the bush until they reach the immediate vicinity of the camp-fires, in front of which the girls they are in search of are sleeping. Slowly and silently, they creep close enough to distinguish the figure of one of those leubras; then one of the intruders stretches out his spear, and inserts its barbed point amongst her thick flowing locks; turning the spear slowly round, some of her hair speedily becomes entangled with it; then, with a sudden jerk, she is aroused from her slumber, and as her eyes open, she feels the sharp point of another weapon pressed against her throat. She neither faints nor screams; she knows well that the slightest attempt at escape or alarm will cause her instant death, so, like a sensible woman, she makes a virtue of necessity, and rising silently, she follows her captors. They lead her away to a considerable distance, tie her to a tree, and return to ensnare their other victim in like manner. Then, when they have accomplished their design, they hurry off to their own camp, where they are received with universal applause, and highly honoured for their *gallant* exploit. Occasionally an alarm is given, but even then the wife-stealers easily escape amidst the confusion, to renew their attempt at some future period. When a distinguished warrior carries off a bride from a strange tribe, he will frequently volunteer to undergo 'the trial of spears,' in order to prevent the necessity of his people going to war in his defence; then both the tribes meet, and ten of their smartest and strongest young men are picked out by the aggrieved party. These are each provided with three reed-spears, and a *wommera*, or throwing-stick; and the offender, armed only with his *heiliman* (a bark-shield eighteen inches long by six wide), is led out in front, and placed at the distance of forty yards. Then, at a given signal, the thirty spears are launched at him in rapid succession; these he receives and parries with his shield, and so skilful are the blacks in the use of their own weapons, that very seldom is any wound inflicted. Having successfully passed through this ordeal, the warrior is considered to have fairly earned his leubra, and to have atoned for his offence in carrying her off; so the ceremony generally concludes by the two tribes feasting together in perfect harmony."

It is impossible, in reading this account of the Australian mode of capturing women, not to recall what Plutarch says of the ceremonies of Roman marriage, apropos of the Rape of the Sabines:—"It is a custom still observed for the bride not to go over the threshold of her husband's house herself, but to be carried over; (compare additional example of the Form No. 5, p. 119), because the Sabine virgins did not go in voluntarily, but were carried in by violence. *Some add that the bride's hair is parted with the point of a spear, in memory of the first marriages being brought about in a warlike manner."*

2. *Probable Origin of the Name Racshasa.*—We saw (p. 34) that, in the code of Menu, one of the eight legal forms of the marriage ceremony was that by capture *de facto,* and called Racshasa, and that this marriage was permitted to the military class. It is curious that the name of this species of marriage should be that of a race of beings—the Rakshasas—whom we find playing an important part, and that connected with a legend of a capture, in the mythic history of the Hindus. The story of the Ramayana may be said to be that of the carrying off of Rama's wife, Sita, by the Rakshasa, Ravana, and of the consequent war carried on by Rama against the Rakshasas, ending in their defeat and the recovery of Sita (See [Monier-] Williams's "Indian Epic Poetry," pp. 74–76). Wilson ("India Three Thousand Years Ago"; Bombay, 1858, p. 20) speaks of the Rakshasas as "a people, often alluded to, from whom the Aryas suffered much, and who, by their descendants, were transferred in idea to the most distant south, and treated by them as a race of mythical giants." He ranks them with the Dasyus, Ugras, Pishachas, and Asuras, as indigenous barbarian races or tribes, which had to be overcome before the Aryans could effect a settlement in part of Hindustan. Lassen takes the same view. "The Ramayana," he says (Lassen, vol. i. p. 535; we quote from Muir's "Sanskrit Texts," vol. ii. p. 425) "contains the narrative of the first attempt of the Aryans to extend themselves to the south by conquest; but it presupposes the peaceable extension of Brahmanical missions in the same direction as having taken place still earlier. . . . The Rakshasas, who are represented as disturbing the sacrifices and devouring the priests, signify here, as often elsewhere, merely the savage tribes which placed themselves in hostile opposition to the Brahmanical institutions. The only other actors who appear in the legend, in addition to these inhabitants, are the monkeys, which ally themselves to Rama and render him assistance. This can only mean that, when the Arian Kshatriyas first made hostile incursions into the south, they were aided by another portion of the indigenous tribes." Dr. Muir can find no authority for saying that the word Rakshasa was originally the name of a tribe. At the same time ("Texts," vol. ii. p. 434), he inclines to hold the descriptions we have of them as having more probably originated in hostile contact with the savages of the south, than as the simple offspring of the poet's imagination. He notices ("Texts," vol. ii. p. 426) that, even in the Vedic period,

the Rakshasas "had been magnified into demons and giants by the poetical and superstitious imaginations of the early (Arian) bards." He quotes from the Ramayana a passage which represents them as cannibals—feeding on blood, men-devouring, changing their shapes, etc.; and another, in which they are described as "of fearful swiftness and unyielding in battle"; while Ravana, the most terrible of all the Rakshasas, is stigmatised as a "destroyer of religious duties, and ravisher of the wives of others." Dr. Muir adds, that the description of the Rakshasas in the Ramayana "corresponds in many respects with the epithets applied to the same class of beings (whether we take them for men or for demons) who are so often alluded to in the Rigveda," and that it is quite possible that the author of the Ramayana may have borrowed therefrom many of the traits which he ascribes to the Rakshasas.

But how came the name of a legal mode of marriage to be that of such a race of beings? The only answer that we can make is a surmise—viz., that while the system of capture had not as yet died out among the Kshatriyas, or warrior caste of the Aryans, it was perfect among the races to which the name Rakshasas was applied; and that what was *their* system gave its designation to the exceptional, although permitted, marriage by capture among the Kshatriyas. This is the more probable, since, so far as we can ascertain, there is nothing in the name—Rakshasa—itself, descriptive of the mode of marriage.

From another point of view, it may be observed that the Rakshasas hold nearly the same place in Hindu tradition that giants, ogres, and trolls occupy in Scandinavian and Celtic legends. They are supernatural beings—robbers and plunderers of human habitations—men-devourers and women-stealers. The giants and ogres of the north share the characteristics of Ravana. The cruel monsters are always carrying off kings' daughters. As Rama's exploits culminate in the recovery of Sita, so the northern giant-slayer is crowned with the greatest glory when he has rescued the captive princesses and restored them in safety to the king's—their father's—palace. Are we to hold all such beings—giants, ogres, trolls, etc.—wherever they occur, as representing savage races, between whom and the peoples in whose legends they appear, as supernatural beings, there was chronic hostility?

3. *Africa.*—The following is the account which poor Speke received from the Queen of Uganda regarding marriage there:— "There are no such things as marriages in Uganda: there are no cere-

monies attached to it. If any Mkungu possessed of a pretty daughter committed an offence, he might give her to the king as a peace-offering; if any neighbouring king had a pretty daughter, and the king of Uganda wanted her, she might be demanded as a fitting tribute. The Wakungu in Uganda are supplied with women by the king, according to their merits, from seizures in battle abroad, or seizures from refractory officers at home. The women are not regarded as property according to the Wanyamŭézi practice, though many exchange their daughters; and some women, for misdemeanours, are sold into slavery; whilst others are flogged, or are degraded to do all the menial services of the house"—(Speke's "Journal," etc., 1863, p. 361).

Bibliography of Works Cited

Achilles Tatius. *The Loves of Clitophon and Leucippe.*

Archaeologia Americana. See Gallatin, Albert.

Archer, Edward C. 1833. *Tours in Upper India, and in Parts of the Himalaya Mountains, with Accounts of the Courts of the Native Princes, etc.* 2 vols. London.

Aristotle. *Politics.*

Asiatick Researches, vol. 3. *See* Eliot, John.

Asiatick Researches, vol. 5. *See* Duncan, Jonathan.

"Australian Blacks." 1864. *Chambers' Journal of Popular Literature, Science and Arts* no. 43 (22 October): 686–88. London & Edinburgh.

Bates, Henry Walter. 1864. *The Naturalist on the River Amazons,* 2d ed. London.

Bell, James Stanislaus. 1840. *Journal of a Residence in Circassia during the years 1837, 1838, 1839.* 2 vols. London.

Bergmann, Benjamin F. B. 1804. *Benjamin Bergmann's nomadische Streife reien unter den Kalmüker in der Jahren 1802 und 1803.* 4 vols. Riga.

Book of Days. See Chambers, R., ed.

Buchanan, Francis. 1807. *A Journey from Madras through the Countries of Mysore, Canara and Malabar.* 3 vols. London.

Bunsen, Christian Carl Josias von. 1813. *De Jure Hereditario Atheniensium disquisitio philologica.* Gottingen.

Burckhardt, John Lewis. 1830. *Notes on the Bedouins and Wahábys.* Edited by Sir William Ouseley. London.

Caesar, Caius Julius. *De Bello Gallico.*

Campbell, John. 1864. *A Personal Narrative of Thirteen Years Service amongst the Wild Tribes of Khondistan for the Suppression of Human Sacrifice*. London.

Campbell, Walter. 1864. *My Indian Journal*. Edinburgh.

Chambers, R., ed. 1863. *The Book of Days*. London and Edinburgh.

Chambers' Journal. See "Australian Blacks."

Clarke, Edward Daniel. 1816. *Travels in Various Countries of Europe, Asia, and Africa*. London.

Cochrane, John Dundas. 1825. *Narrative of a Pedestrian Journey through Russia and Siberian Tartary, from the Frontiers of China to the Frozen Sea and Kamtchatka; Performed during the Years 1820, 1821, 1822 and 1823*. 2 vols. London.

Cunningham, Sir Alexander. 1854. *Ladák, Physical, Statistical, and Historical; with Notices of the Surrounding Countries*. London.

Dobrizhoffer, Martinus. 1822. *An Account of the Abipones, an Equestrian People of Paraguay*. Translated by Sara Coleridge. 3 vols. London.

Duncan, Jonathan. 1798. "Historical Remarks on the Coast of Malabar, with Some Description of Its Inhabitants," *Asiatick Researches* 5:1–36.

Eliot, John. 1792. "Observations on the Inhabitants of the Garrow Hills, Made during a Public Deputation in the Years 1788–1789," *Asiatick Researches* 3:17–37.

Elphinstone, The Hon. Mountstuart. 1815. *An Account of the Kingdom of Caubal and Its Dependencies in Persia, Tartary, and India*. London.

Erman, Georg Adolph. 1848. *Travels in Siberia*. Translated by W. D. Cooley. 2 vols.

Erskine, John Elphinstone. 1853. *Journal of a Cruise among the Islands of the Western Pacific*. London.

Festus, Sextus Pompeius. *De Verborum Significatione.*

Fisher (Captain). 1840. "Memoir of Sylhet, Kachar, and the Adjacent Districts." *Journal of the Asiatic Society* (Calcutta) 9:808–43.

Fitzroy, Robert. 1839. *Narrative of the Surveying Voyages of His Majesty's Ships* Adventurer *and* Beagle, *between the Years 1826 and 1836*. 3 vols. London.

Forbes, Jonathan. 1840. *Eleven Years in Ceylon.* 2 vols. London.

Fraser, James Baillie. 1838. *A Winter's Journey from Constantinople to Tehran; with Travels through Various Parts of Persia.* 2 vols. London.

Gallatin, Albert. 1836. "A Synopsis of the Indian Tribes of North America." *Archaeologia Americana, Transactions and Collections of the American Antiquarian Society* (Worcester, Mass.) 2:1–422.

Gaya, Louis de. 1698. *Marriage Ceremonies.* London.

Goguet, Antoine Yves. 1761. *The Origin of Laws, Arts, and Sciences and Their Progress among the Most Ancient Nations.* 3 vols. Edinburgh.

Grant, James. 1814. *Thoughts on the Origin and Descent of the Gael.* Edinburgh.

Grey, Sir George. 1841. *Journals of Two Expeditions of Discovery in North-West and Western Australia, during the years 1837, 38, and 39.* 2 vols. London.

———. 1855. *Polynesian Mythology, and the Ancient Traditional History of the New Zealand Race As Furnished by Their Priests and Chiefs.* London.

Grote, George. 1862. *A History of Greece.* 8 vols. London.

Hamilton, Alexander. 1727. *New Account of the East Indies, Being the Remarks of Capt. A.H. Who Spent His Time There from 1688 to 1723.* 2 vols. Edinburgh.

Haxthausen, August von. 1854. *Transcaucasia: Sketches of the Natives and Races between the Black Sea and the Caspian.* London.

Herodotus. 1862. *History of Herodotus.* A new English version edited by George Rawlinson. 4 vols. London.

Home, Sir Henry. 1807. *Sketches of the History of Man.* 3 vols. Edinburgh.

Hommaire de Hell, Xavier. 1847. *Travels in the Steppes of the Caspian Sea, the Crimea, the Caucasus, etc.* London.

Huc, Evariste Régis. 1852. *Travels in Tartary, Thibet, and China, during the Years 1844–5–6.* Translated by W. Hazlitt. 2 vols. London.

Humboldt, Friedrich Heinrich Alexander von. 1819. *Personal Narrative of Travels to the Equinoctial Regions of the New Continent during the Years 1799–1804.* Translated by H. M. Williams. 7 vols. London.

Institutes of Menu. See Jones, Sir William.

Irish Version of Nennius. See Todd, J. H.

Jackson, John. 1853. "Narrative by John Jackson of His Residence in the Feejees." In Erskine, appendix A, pp. 411–77.

Jones, Sir William, trans. 1863. *Mánava Dharma Sástra or the Institutes of Manu According to the Gloss of Kullaka.* Madras.

Kames. *See* Home, Sir Henry.

Kleuker, Johann Friedrich. 1777. *Zend-avesta.* 3 vols. Riga.

Krusenstern, Adam Johann von. 1813. *Voyage round the World, in the Years 1803, 1804, 1805, and 1806.* Translated by A. B. Hoppner. 2 vols. London.

Lang, John Dunmore. 1839. "Letter to Dr. T. Hodgkin." *Extracts from the Papers and Proceedings of the Aborigines Protection Society* (London) 5 (October and November): 140–42.

La Pérouse, Jean François de Galaup. 1798. *A Voyage round the World.* 2 vols. London.

Lassen, Christian. 1847–62. *Indische Alterthumskunde.* 4 vols. Bonn and Leipzig.

Latham, Robert Gordon. 1859. *Descriptive Ethnology.* 2 vols. London.

Lewis, Thomas. 1724–25. *Origines Hebraeae: The Antiquities of the Hebrew Republick.* 4 vols. London.

Livingstone, David. 1857. *Missionary Travels and Researches in South Africa.* London.

McCulloch, William. 1859. *Account of the Valley of Munnipore and of the Hill Tribes.* Calcutta.

MacPherson, Samuel Charters. 1842. *Report upon the Khonds of the Districts of Ganjam and Cuttack.* Calcutta.

———. 1852. "An Account of the Religion of the Khonds in Orissa," *Journal of the Royal Asiatic Society Great Britain and Ireland* (London) 13:216–74.

Magnus, Johannes. 1554. *Gothorum Sueonumque Historia.* Rome.

Magnus, Olaus. 1555. *Historia de Gentibus Septentrionalibus.* Rome.

Maine, Sir Henry James Summer. 1861. *Ancient Law.* London.

Mandeville, Sir John. *The Voiage and Travaile of Sir. I. Mandeville.* (McLennan used a version based on the 1725 edition.)

Monier-Williams, Sir Monier. 1863. *Indian Epic Poetry.* London and Edinburgh.

Moorcroft, William, and Trebeck, George. 1841. *Travels in the Himalayan Provinces of Hindustan and the Punjab; in Ladakh and Kashmir; in Peshawar, Kabul, Kunduz and Bokhara from 1819 to 1825.* Prepared for the press from original journals and correspondence by H. H. Wilson. 2 vols. London.

Morgan, Lewis Henry. 1860. Circular letter and schedules included in "The Welsh Indians," *The Cambrian Journal* (Tenby) 3 (2ds.): 142–58.

Moser, Ludwig. 1856. *The Caucasus and Its People.* London.

Müller, Carl Otfried. 1830. *The History and Antiquities of the Doric Race.* Translated by Henry Tufnell and Sir George Cornewall Lewis. 2 vols. Oxford.

Müller, Friedrich Max. 1859. *History of Ancient Sanskrit Literature.* London.

Muir, John. 1860. "The Trans-Himalayan Origin of the Hindus, and Their Affinity with the Western Branches of the Asian Race." *Original Sanskrit Texts on the Origin and History of the People of India, Their Religion and Institutions.* 2. London.

Pallas, Peter Simon. 1794. *Voyages dans plusieurs provinces de l' Empire de Russie et dans l'Asie septentrionale.* Paris.

Paulus, Julius. *Julii Pauli receptarum sententiarum.*

Philo, Judaeus. 1854–55. *The Works of Philo Judaeus; the Contemporary of Josephus.* Translated by C. D. Yonge. 4 vols. London.

Piers, Sir Henry. 1682. "A chorographical description of the County of West-Meath." *Collectanea de rebus Hibernicis* (Dublin). Edited by Charles Vallancey. 1:1–126.

Plutarch. *Life of Lycurgus.*

Polo, Marco. 1854. *The Travels of Marco Polo, the Venetian.* "Bohn's Antiquarian Library." Edited by T. Wright. London.

Prasannakumāra Thākura. 1863. *Vivada Chintamani.* Calcutta.

Prichard, James Cowles. 1855. *The Natural History of Man*. Edited by Edwin Norris. 2 vols. London.

Reade, William Winwood. 1863. *Savage Africa*. London.

Secondat, Charles Louis de, Baron de Montesquieu. *The Spirit of Laws*.

Selden, John. 1640. *De Jure Naturali et Gentium juxta disciplinam Ebraeorum. Libri Septem*. London.

Skene, William F., ed. 1867. *Chronicles of the Picts, Chronicles of the Scots, and Other Early Memorials of Scottish History*. Edinburgh. (McLennan obtained information contained in this work from its editor prior to is publication.)

Smith, William, ed. 1860–63. *A Dictionary of the Bible*. 3 vols. London.

Solinus, Caius Julius. 1848. "Polyhistoriae." *Monumenta Historica Brittanica*. Edited by Henry Petrie. London.

Speke, John Hanning. 1863. *Journal of the Discovery of the Source of the Nile*. Edinburgh and London.

Spencer, Edmund. 1837. *Travels in Circassia, Krim Tartary, etc.* 2 vols. London.

Strabo. 1707. *Geografia*. Amsterdam.

Strahlenberg, Philip Johan. 1736. *A Histori-geographical Description of the Northern and Eastern Part of Europe and Asia*. London.

Suidas. 1705. *Suidae Lexicon, Graece et Latine*. 3 vols. Cambridge.

Tacitus, Publius Cornelius. 1851. *The Germania of Tacitus*. Edited by R. G. Latham. London.

Tanner, John. 1830. *A Narrative of the Captivity and Adventures of John Tanner during 30 Years Residence among the Indians in the Interior of North America*. Edited by Edwin James. New York.

Tennent, Sir James Emerson. 1859. *Ceylon*. 2 vols. London.

Tod, James. 1829–32. *Annals and Antiquities of Rajast'han*. 2 vols. London.

———. 1839. *Travels in Western India*. London.

Todd, J. H., ed. 1848. *The Irish Version of the Historia Britonum of Nennius*. Dublin.

Turnbull, John. 1805. *A Voyage round the World in the Years 1800–1804.* 3 vols. London.

Turner, Samuel. 1800. *An Account of an Embassy to the Court of the Teshoo Lama, in Tibet.* London.

Vallancey, Charles. 1786. *Collectanea de rebus Hibernicis.* Dublin.

Varro, apud Aurelius Augustinus. *De Civitate Dei.*

Vigne, Godfrey Thomas. 1842. *Travels in Kashmir, Ladak, Iskards, the Countries Adjoining the Mountain-course of the Indus, and the Himalaya, North of Punjab.* 2 vols. London.

Vivada Chintamani. See Prasannakumāra Thākura.

Volney, Constantin François de. 1787. *Travels through Syria and Egypt in the Years 1783, 1784, and 1785.* 2 vols. London.

Weber, Albrecht, ed. 1862. *Indische Studien.* Berlin.

Weinhold, Karl. 1851. *Die deutschen Frauen in dem Mittelalter.* Vienna.

Williams. *See* Monier-Williams.

Wilson of Mussoorie. 1860. *A Summer Ramble in the Himalayas.* London.

Wilson, John. 1858. *India Three Thousand Years Ago; or, the Social State of A'ryas on the Banks of the Indus in the Times of the Vedas.* Bombay.

Xenophon. *On the Lacedaemonian Republic.*

Xiphilinus, Joannes. 1848. "Epitomes Dionis Cassii." *Monumenta Historica Britannica.* Edited by H. Petrie. London.

Index

Aron, 88

Abipones, 52

Abraham, married to his sister-german, 65, 88, 98

Achaeans, 12

Achilles Tatius, 88, 127

Adoption, Act of, 9; fiction of, 94; fiction of, as origin of heterogeneity, 109; Libripens present at, 9

Aenezes, form of capture among, 81, 118

Affections: domestic, 55; filial, 63; fraternal, 63; social, 55; unselfish, 67

Affghanistan, practice of capturing wives in, 28

Africa, 6, 18, 19, 27, 38, 44, 72, 73, 84, 86; defective information respecting, 38; form of capture in, 18; marriage in equatorial, 124

Agathyrsi, said to have had wives in common, 72

Agnates, definition of, 94

Agnatic: groups, xxxiv, 105, 108–9; kinship, 62, 95, 102, 110, 111; relationships, 6, 94–95, 99, 100, 112, 113

Agnation, 48 n, 83, 91, 92, 94, 95, 103, 104, 114–15; as concomitant of patriarchal system, 91; effect of, 99–101; as familiar system, 94–95, 98, 99; growth of, 93–99

Aimak, absence of conjugal fidelity among, 72 n

Alba, 36

Aleutian Islands, polyandry in, 73, 75

Amazons, the, 26, 27

America, 6, 18, 19, 26, 27, 37–38, 73, 93, 100

American Indians, 19, 28, 51 n, 79, 85, 88; anciently polyandrous, 85; exogamous, 50; practice of capturing wives among, 26–28; system of kinship through females only among, 51 n, 85; traces of the form of capture among, 18. *See also* North American Indians; South American Indians

Amram, married to his father's sister, 88

Ancient Law. See Maine, H. J. S.

Angom (family of Munniepore tribe), 46–47

Animals, men as gregarious, 67

Ansariens, said to have wives in common, 72 n

Anthropological Society, xi

Apparel, bridal, 13, 119

Apuleius, 13

Aquapim, kinship through females only in, 86

Arabs, 16, 72 n, 83, 119, 123; form of capture among, 16, 119. *See also* Bedouin Arabs; Mezeyne

Archaeologia Americana. See Gallatin

Archer, E. C., 73 n, 79 n, 127

Aristotle, 108 n, 127

Arts, invention of, 67

Aryan civilization, 88; institutions, 6

135

140

betan form of, 71, 74–75, 76, 77, 78, 79–80, 82–84, 85, 88, 96–97; less rude, and its relationship to male kinship, 78, 80, 99; among lower classes, 75; origin of, 68, 71, 84; its relationship with exogamy, 85 n, 91; its relationship with forms of descent, 71–72, 75, 83; relationship terminology associated with, 85, 88; ruder, lower, of Nair form of, 71, 74–75, 76, 77–78, 79, 82–83, 84, 90, 96, 97; ruder, and its relationship to kinship through females, 75, 84, 90, 115; as stage in Aryan civilization, 88; as stage of human progress, 79, 84, 90; stages of decay of less rude form, 80–84, 98; test for detecting previous existence of, 74, 80

Polygamy, 48, 49, 72 n, 77, 97–98
Polygunia, 74, 84, 86, 104, 105
Portuguese, the, 27
Possessions. See Property
Pothier, 13 n
Potowottomies, 51 n
Preface of general history, the, 6–7
Prasannakumāra Thākura, 45 n, 131
Prichard, J. C., 49 n, 132
Primitive age, 9, 22–23, 30
Primitive groups: homogeneous, 61, 92; state of war between, 25; structure of, 4, 92–94
Primitive life, importance of knowledge of, 5–7
Primitive Marriage: argument, xxii–xxvii; criticism of, xxxviii–xl; development of theory of, xxvii–xxxvi; method of, xliii–xliv; notes on new edition of, xlv–xlvi; scope of, xl–xliii; sources of, xl. See also McLennan, John F.
Primitive races, 5, 7, 18, 19, 29
Primitive state, fundamental error concerning, 107
Primogeniture, law of, 52 n, 96, 97
Professions, as origin of caste divisions, 102 n

Progress, human, 5, 6, 7, 28, 65, 66, 67
Promiscuity, 66–67, 69, 70, 71, 72, 85, 87 n; general, 69, 70, 72, 84; indifference to, 69; incestuous, 90; less general or modified, 70; modern examples of, 72 n; regulated (see Polyandry)
Property, 20, 22, 69, 77, 78, 80–81, 96, 98; children as, 99; common rights in, 78, 112; family, 112; gens, 111, 112; group, 69, 112; history of, 67, 112; individual, 47, 112; wives as, 98–99
Proserpine. See Pluto
Prudery, false reason for marriage by capture, 11–12
Prussia, transitional form of capture in, 30
Puharies (of Gurwhal), 72 n, 85, 88
Purity, indifference to marital, 72 n

Queen. See Uganda, queen of

Races, history of, 5, 7, 9, 11, 18, 19, 28, 38, 48 n, 56, 60, 65, 67, 72, 88
Racshasa, 34; origin of name of, 123–25. See also Institutes of Menu
Rajputs, 61, 74, 86
Rakshasas, 123–25
Rama. See Ramayana, story of the
Ramayana, story of the, 4, 123–25
Rape, act of, 20, 23, 33, 100; of the Cruithnians, 52; of the Gael by the Picts, 36; pretence of, 20; of the Sabines, 11, 36, 37, 122; by Theseus, 35
Ravana. See Ramayana, story of the
Rawlinson's Notes. See Herodotus
Reade, W. W., 72 n, 73 n, 86 n, 132
Regime, dysharmonic, 49
Reish-suffeeds, 118
Religion, 12 n, 58; feud associated with, 104; infanticide as institute